786.3
Sto

Stormen, Win.

Popular piano
self-taught

POPULAR PIANO
Self-Taught

Win Stormen

Bonanza Books
New York

ACKNOWLEDGMENTS

To Milton Gladstone, who decided to bring this book to the attention of the world when it was two chapters and a brief outline; to the editors of Arco who patiently deciphered my somewhat mysterious handwriting; and to my music typographers, who did their job well considering the circumstances.

I would also like to again thank W.C. Handy, Handy Brothers Inc., who gave me permission to use part of "St. Louis Blues" in earlier editions of this book.

This 1984 edition is published by Bonanza Books, distributed by Crown Publishers, Inc. by arrangement with Arco Publishing.

Manufactured in the United States of America

Library of Congress Cataloging in Publication Data

Stormen, Win.
    Popular piano self-taught.

    Reprint. Originally published: New York : Arco Pub.
Co., 1982.
    Includes index.
    1. Piano—Methods—Self-instruction. 2. Piano—
Methods (Rock) 3. Rock music—Instruction and study.
I. Title.
MT248.S84 1984   786.3'041   84-21588
    ISBN: 0-517-460017
h g f e d c

TABLE OF CONTENTS

CHAPTER

Author's Preface

It was a most pleasant surprise when my publishers asked me to revise *Popular Piano Self-Taught*. It has been several years since the initial publication, and a revision at this time will certainly bring everything up to date.

Today, it is important that we become acquainted with as many styles of popular piano as possible. There is no *one* way to play a popular song. So much depends on the kind of song it is (popular, disco, rock, western, blues, etc...) and *how* we would like to hear it sound. This is what makes popular music so appealing and fascinating. We can make our own arrangements of songs, as we please. We are not restricted to what is written on the piano part of sheet music. We can even take a classical theme and make our own arrangements, as I have done with Dvorak's *New World Symphony* theme (sometimes known as "Going Home").

In this new edition I have also added many new songs and new rock and roll and disco sections. I hope my readers will be pleased with these new additions.

The piano is still the most popular of all musical instruments. Simple arrangements of keyboard tones and the ease of playing the tones are two prime reasons for its mass appeal. The easy, somewhat mechanical structure of popular piano music has reduced the learning process to simple step-by-step procedures that have attracted more adherents than almost any other musical instrument. Indeed, it is possible to learn the art of popular piano playing without supervision by an instructor.

If you apply yourself to the materials in this book, you will soon find yourself playing in simple, colorful styles. True, you will not sound like Art Tatum or George Shearing, but you will derive high personal satisfaction. If you conscientiously apply yourself to the materials covered, you will find that by the end of the first and second chapters you will be playing well known folk and popular songs with both hands—even in as little time as a few hours. Later, you will be introduced to Rock and Roll and Disco, and all other chords used in popular music; to syncopated rhythms; and to the easy breaks and runs that color popular songs.

It is important to follow the advice on the next page to achieve maximum results. This is your book now. Use it well, and it will be a happy experience.

Win Stormen

General Usage of This Book

At the outset, it is advisable to proceed slowly. If you are a beginner, learning one or two chapters a day would be sufficient. Those, of course, who know the fundamentals of music can cover the material faster. The exercises illustrated in the book should be practiced as shown in all chapters. Consequently, access to a piano is important. Whether the piano is your own, your neighbor's, or the property of the local club house, use it as frequently as possible. The only set routine is to read through the material steadily, without allowing too much time to elapse between reading intervals.

The playing of all exercises and examples will help you learn songs since most of the chords, scales and other material can be found in the various songs reproduced in this book.

I would like to recommend the Pop Piano Keyboard Grip Exercises, in Chapter 16, as a warm-up and/or a steady exercise to keep your fingers agile.

CHAPTER 1
THE EARLY STAGES

In order to understand and play popular music, we must first learn the following basic essentials that underlie all music instruction.

All musical notation is built upon a *staff*. The *staff*, as shown in the following example, consists of five lines and four spaces:

The medium and high notes in music are written in the *treble clef* (usually referred to as the G Clef in classical music). The signature notation for the *treble clef* is on the extreme left of the staff:

The lower tones in music are written in the *bass clef* (or F Clef in classical music). Its signature notation is also on the extreme left of the staff:

Notes placed on lines in the *treble clef* are:

Notes placed in spaces in the *treble clef* are:

Notes placed in spaces in the *bass clef* are:

Notes placed on lines in the *bass clef* are:

Notice that the letter formations in the *bass clef* start with the second letter of the *treble clef* and continue in a similar manner, except for the last line and the last space, which is A and G, respectively. All Bass Clef tones are the same as Treble Clef tones except that they are one line lower (for notes on lines) and one space lower (for notes in spaces).

The treble and bass clefs are separated by an *imaginary* line with Middle C at its center. Let us take a brief glance at the clefs to see how they are constructed.

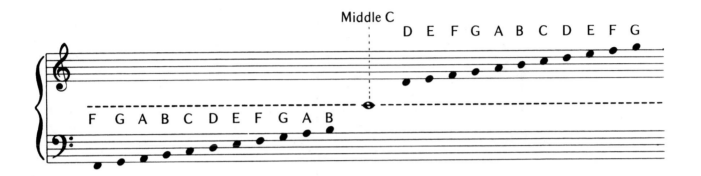

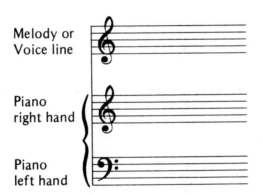

The melody line, consisting of single melody notes, is written on the top *treble clef.*

The *treble* and *bass clefs* within brackets indicate the piano part. At present, to simplify our piano instruction, we will only use the top treble clef.

Later we will see how the two lower clefs are combined so that the right and left hands can be played together, with the right hand playing the treble clef and the left hand the bass clef.

Lines called *ledger lines* may be added to notes falling above or below the *staff*.

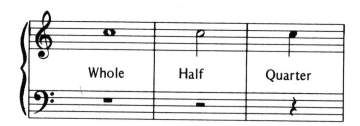

Time Values

The form of a note determines its time value. The following is a table of time values for notes and rests:

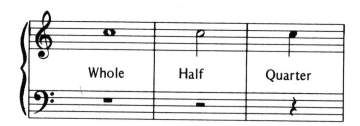

Each note is played and held in relation to its respective time value and time signature. This will be illustrated shortly.

Notes and rests having less time value than a quarter note are notated on the following page.

| Eighth | Sixteenth |

A dot placed after a note or rest adds one-half to the time value of the note or rest. A second dot adds one-half to the time value of the first dot. The example below is further illustrated on page 10.

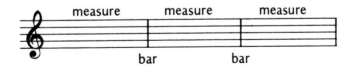

A slur connecting the heads of two identical notes, indicates the notes are tied:

Only the first note is played. The time value is equivalent to the sum of the two notes. In the above example, the tied half notes equal a whole note. For tied notes in syncopation, see page 70.

Music Division

Music is divided into *measures* by vertical bar lines:

measure   measure   measure

bar   bar

Each measure has a given number of notes and beats. A beat is a pulse or count that divides a measure into equal divisions of time. If, for example, we allow two beats per measure, we can divide each beat into a second, thus giving an exact time limit to each beat. See Example A on the next page.

The given number of beats or notes to a measure is determined by the *time signature.*

Time Signatures

Following are some of the various signatures used in popular music:

Two Quarter Time: $\frac{2}{4}$

Two Quarter Time is found occasionally in popular sheet music. It is the signature used in novelty songs, early ragtime, and musical comedy songs that have a very fast tempo. It is usually notated as follows:

Two Quarter Time has two beats to a measure, each beat equal to a quarter note. Counting two beats to a measure gives us:

Example A

If we allow two seconds per measure, we can divide each note into the following number of seconds.

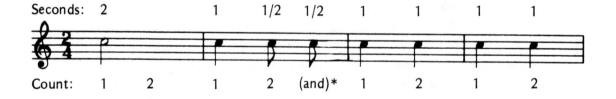

This example tells you how long to hold each note. It can be observed that:

*see page 7

All *half notes* (♩) are held for two beats or two seconds.

All *quarter notes* (♩) are held for one beat or one second.

All *eighth notes* (♪) are one-half the time value of quarter notes and are held only half as long, or for one-half second. Therefore, the two eighth notes in the second bar on the preceding page equal one beat or one second. To help in counting, you may say "and" when an eighth note is a division of a beat. (See example preceding page.)

Four Quarter Time

Four Quarter Time is the notation for Rock and Disco music.

Four Quarter Time has four beats to a measure, each beat equal to a quarter note.

Counting four beats to a measure gives us:

    1 2 3 4   1 2 3 4   1 2 3 4   1 2 3   4   1 2 3 4

One form of Four Quarter Time used in popular songs that move at a fast tempo (with four beats to a measure, each beat equal to a quarter note) is notated as follows:

The Keyboard

With six pages of theory behind us, we have now passed the first mark. The next step is to see where the notes lie on the keyboard. Notice that the piano keyboard below consists of black and white keys. The black keys will be explained later. The white keys are illustrated as follows:

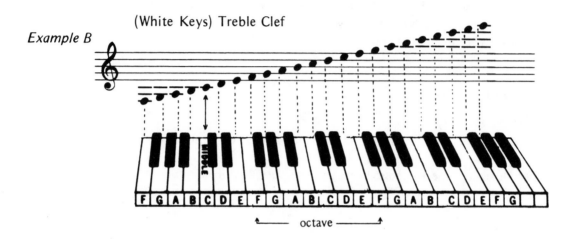

Example B

(White Keys) Treble Clef

F G A B C D E F G A B C D E F G A B C D E F G

←—— octave ——→

Notice the arrow pointing to *Middle C.* Middle C will be our guide for locating the various notes on the keyboard. To find it, count twenty-four white keys from the left side of the keyboard, beginning with the first white key. Middle C will be the twenty-fourth note.

Here are a few observations:

1. There are only seven different letter names for all the white keys. Counting up or down the keyboard, and then starting on any given note, the eighth note will repeat the first. This is known as an *Octave.*

   Using a finger from each hand, press down both notes together as indicated in Example B. Notice the hollow sound of the Octave.

2. The notes to the right of Middle C increase in pitch. Notes to the left decrease in pitch.

3. All notes below F (the fourth note to the left of *Middle C*) are usually written in the Bass Clef.

4. There are five black keys within each Octave.

At this point we can single out the melody line on the keyboard from a few familiar songs, but before doing so, let us do the following:

1. Observe how our fingers are numbered. We will use these numbers on page 13.

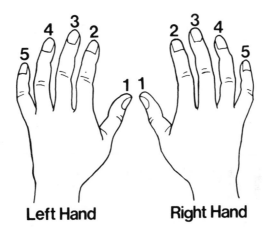

Left Hand   **Right Hand**

2. Observe the correct wrist position in relation to the keyboard.

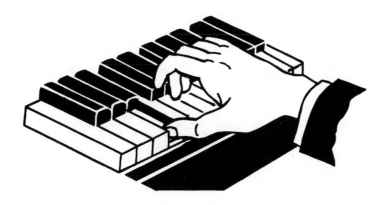

3. Fingers should be slightly curved before perssing down notes with tips of fingers.

4. Your back should be erect, almost perpendicular to the piano bench. Lean forward slightly.

5. Always remember to be in a relaxed state before playing—fingers, wrist, and spine.

Humming the Rhythm

After doing these few simple exercises, you will soon be able to play a melody. First, hum the following note for four beats. As you hum, count in time to yourself 1,2,3,4. Use any sound you can keep time with.

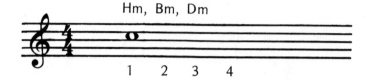

Try humming the following example for half and quarter notes:

Practice the following song, humming and keeping time as above:

Yankee Doodle

Counting Dotted Quarter Notes:

Dotted quarter notes are usually followed by eighth notes.

For dotted quarter notes, we count two beats, then come in at the end of the second beat with the eighth note. Count: one, two and three, four and.

On the eighth note, count "and" twice as fast as the quarter note since the eighth has only half the value. Say "and" quickly, but count it in strict time.

Auld Lang Syne

Try stamping your foot. Count each beat every time you stamp your foot. The "and" will fall between the beat and *not* when you stamp your foot. Keep your foot beat at an even tempo.

Counting Eighth Notes:

In counting eighth notes in pairs, ♪♪(this may also be written ♫), the beat falls on the first note of the pair.

Try the following songs, humming and counting as in the preceding examples:

Long, Long Ago

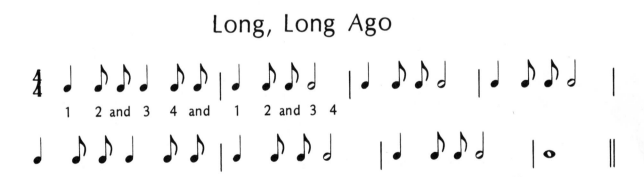

All Through the Night

Traditional Welsh Air

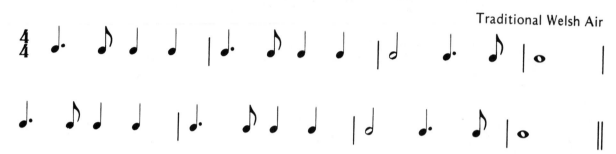

Counting Dotted Half Notes:

Sustain dotted half notes for three beats, in $\frac{4}{4}$.

1 2 3 4

Practice the following song, humming and counting as in the preceding examples:

Red River Valley

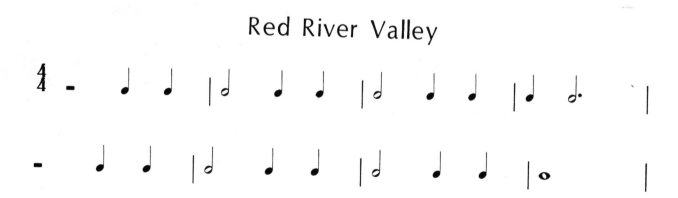

Now try a few bars from *Red River Valley,* using the fingering shown for the right hand on the next page. Remember to press down the notes on the keyboard firmly and to keep an even sound. The numbers under the notes indicate what fingers to use. The keyboard diagram above the notes will aid you in finding notes on the keyboard. Review keyboard posture and wrist position on page 9.

Red River Valley

Traditional Cowboy Song

Three Quarter Time: $\frac{3}{4}$

Continuing with time signatures, we now have Three Quarter Time.

Three Quarter Time has three beats to a measure, each beat equal to a quarter note.

beats per measure:

Many popular songs are written in Three Quarter Time. *Moon River* by Henry Mancini and Johnny Mercer, *What the World Needs Now is Love* by Burt Bacharach and Hal David are two examples.

Songs written in waltz time are also notated in Three Quarter Time, with the accent on the first beat of the bar. The beat for waltz time rhythm is more precise, very unlike the three quarter beat found in popular songs.

Hum and count the following rhythms:

In the next example we have a tied note (see page 70). Remember to hold it for six beats.

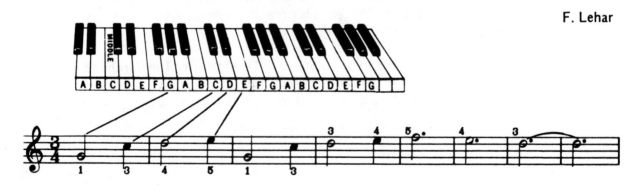

Using the corresponding fingerings, play the following few bars which should give you an idea of the rhythmic scheme in Three Quarter Time.

Merry Widow Waltz

F. Lehar

Popular Music Symbols

Accidentals:

Accidentals used in music notation are the sharp (♯), the flat (♭), and the natural (♮).

A sharp placed before a note raises it one-half step.

A half step is the next succeeding note on the keyboard. In practically all cases the raised tone will be played on a black note.

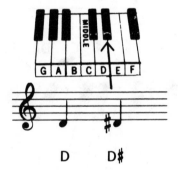

A flat placed before a note lowers it one-half step.

As in sharps, the flatted tone will in *most* cases be played on a black key.

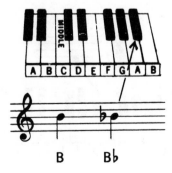

A natural cancels any preceding accidentals, (sharp or flat) within the measure.

The following illustrates the sharps and flats in the treble clef:

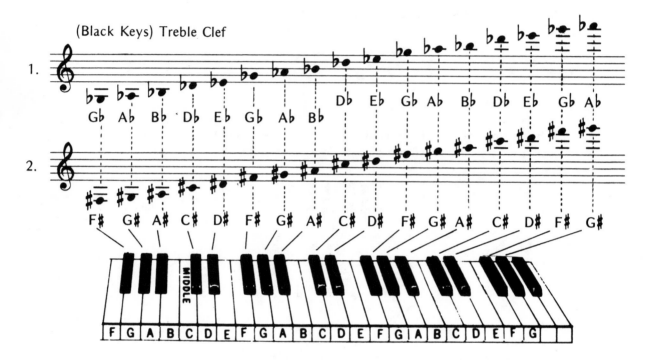

The notes on line 1 and line 2 are the *same*. The difference is in the notation. Here it can be seen that notes *identical in sound* are *different when spelled out on paper.*

The excerpt on the next page illustrates the use of F♯. Notice also F♯ in the sixth measure. Play in time using proper fingering.

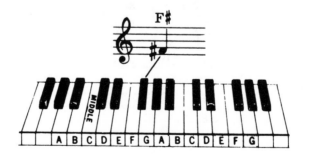

Try playing 1st line
without guide lines
on keyboard:

Teodora Cottrau

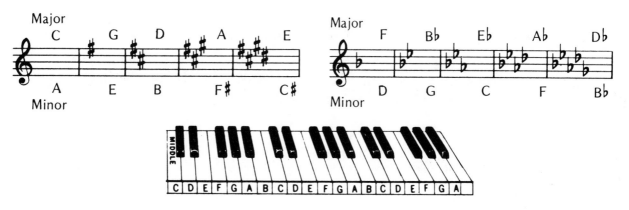

Note
Guide: E   A   G   G F♯ F♮   F   E   D   A   G

Key Signatures

Here are the key signatures used in popular music. The keys of F, C, G, E♭, B♭, A♭, D♭ major and A, E, B, D, G, C, F minor are those keys used most frequently in popular music.

Major
C   G   D   A   E
A   E   B   F♯   C♯
Minor

Major
F   B♭   E♭   A♭   D♭
D   G   C   F   B♭
Minor

Minor key signatures are the same as a major signature one and a half tones (steps) away.

Double Bars

A pair of dots set against double bars  indicates that a section is to be repeated:

Braces

A brace  indicates that both hands are to be played together.

Right hand

Left hand

Chords

Chords are three or more tones of different pitch sounded together. A variety of sound colors may be heard by using various combinations of notes. Single chords or chord patterns can suggest strength, weakness, tension, nostalgia, or sentiment; (just a few ideas on the powerful effects of chords—of course, there are others).

Diatonic and Chromatic Chords

Chords may be either diatonic or chromatic. Diatonic chords are built upon tones of the major scales. Chromatic chords are altered diatonic chords. We will build chords in the next chapter.

The movement or change from one chord to another is termed chord progression. The chord progressions shown in the following chapters are among the many used in popular, rock, disco, folk music, and musical comedy.

Melody

A melody is an arrangement of musical sounds for voice, instrument, or a group of instruments. Most of the melodies we will work with, however, are in the popular form of thirty-two bars that can be sung, played, or memorized by an average individual.

Chord Notation in Sheet Music

In popular sheet music, melodies are accompanied by chord symbols written above the melody line. These symbols denote the chords to be used in harmonization with that portion of the melody. Example:

CHAPTER 2

BUILDING CHORDS

The chords we will use in this book are built on the major (diatonic) scales in the keys most often found in popular music, *i.e.* the keys of C, G, F, Bb, Eb, Ab, Db.

How To Build a Major Scale Step by Step

Note: All major scales are built as follows: Between the first and second and the second and third notes there are whole steps; between the third and fourth notes there is a half step (no piano key in between—see example); between the fourth and fifth and the sixth and seventh notes there are whole steps; and between the seventh and eighth notes there is a half step. Remember to count the black keys. They are notes.

Major Scales

In the key of G, notice the F♯ in the signature on the extreme left of the staff. This carries through the staff and automatically raises F a half step.

In the key of F, B♭ is carried through, lowering B a half step.

Chords are the foundation for playing popular piano. Knowledge of chords will:

1. simplify sight reading;

2. be a guide for improvising on the piano;

3. enable you to develop a technique for playing be ear as well as by notes;

4. help you to acquire a knowledge of harmony.

Building Chords in the Key of C

As we now know, the chords we will use are built on the tones of the scale. Here is the method for building Diatonic Chords.* First, select a major scale.

To notes on lines, add two notes on consecutive lines above. To notes on spaces, add two notes in consecutive spaces above.

This results in the formation of triads. Each triad has a numeral beneath. The numerals indicate the kind of chord, or quality of chord they represent.

I, IV, and V are major chords.

ii, iii, and vi are minor chords.

vii° is a diminished chord.

Substituting chord letter names for the symbols gives us:

The letter name for the chord is derived from the bottom note of the chord.

Small "m" indicates a minor chord.

A single capital letter (below the triad) indicates a major chord.

dim. indicates a diminished chord.*

To form 7th chords, we add one note on the next line above the triad on lines, and one note in the next space above the triad in spaces. Symbols and chord letter names are as follows:

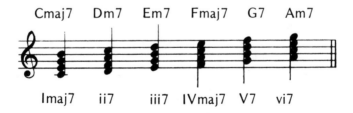

Note: To construct a major triad, we must know that between the bottom note and the middle note there are two whole steps and between the middle and top notes, there is one step and a half. In a minor triad, there are one and a half steps between the bottom and middle notes and two whole steps between the middle and top notes. In the diminished triad, there is a step and a half between the bottom and the middle notes and a step and a half between the middle and the top notes.

*In popular sheet music the diminished triad, as shown above, is seldom used. The diminished 7th chord, a more articulate and larger chord, is used. This is illustrated in Chapter 9.

The Sounds of Chords

The following chords should be played and carefully listened to. Notice the difference in the sound of each chord.

Important: When you play a chord, press down all the notes together.

Play all the notes together of a *Major Chord*. Use the fingering shown.

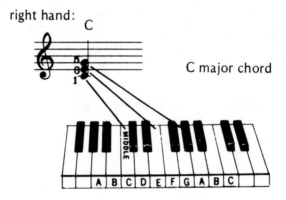

Note the sound of this chord. This is a neutral, strong sound. Compare it to the minor chord below.

Play all the notes together of a *Minor Chord*.

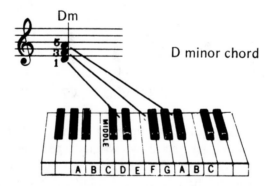

The sound of this chord is somber, and can be recognized by its rather sad, mysterious tone.

Play the *7th chord* on the next page. This is a *Dominant* 7th chord.

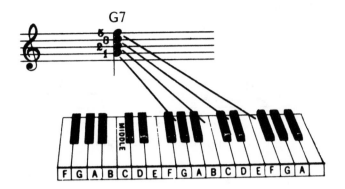

Listen to this sound. It is strong and has a moderate dissonance. Compare this sound to the 7th chord below.

Play the *Major 7th* chord. This is known as the "heartbreak" chord in popular music.

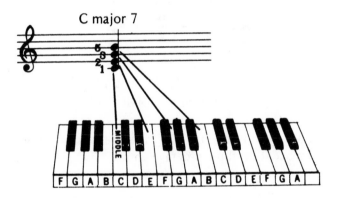

Do you hear the nostalgic, lush quality of this chord? It is often used in popular songs, in ballads describing an emotion of love—new, old . . . or unrequited. A most interesting chord.

Inversions of Chords

An inversion is simply a different position of the same chord as played on the keyboard. To form inversions take the bottom tone of a chord and place it on top of the chord. Selecting three chords, C, F, and G7, let us build inversions of each chord.

First let us start with the C Chord on the next page.

1st inversion of *C chord:*

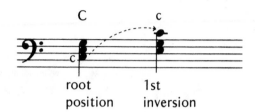

root   1st
position   inversion

In the first inversion, the root of the chord, which is the bottom tone C, is placed an octave above on top of the chord. This automatically forms the 1st inversion of the C chord.

2nd inversion of *C chord:*

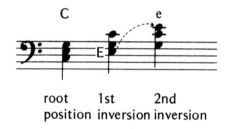

root   1st   2nd
position inversion inversion

To form the second inversion of C, take the bottom tone E from the 1st inversion and place it on top, an octave above.

To hear the sound of the chord, play it with the left hand in the root position and its inversions, using the fingering indicated:

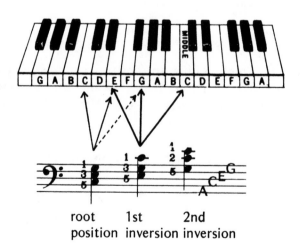

root   1st   2nd
position inversion inversion

Now let us build an *F Chord* and its first inversion:

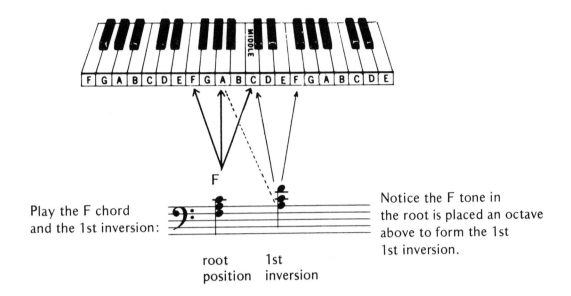

Play the F chord
and the 1st inversion:

root   1st
position   inversion

Notice the F tone in
the root is placed an octave
above to form the 1st
1st inversion.

The G7 chord has three inversions.

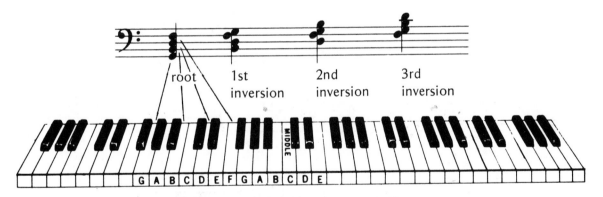

root   1st   2nd   3rd
        inversion   inversion   inversion

Play the above positions of the G7 chord. The root position indicates where
the keyboard tones are in the left hand. Remember, when playing you take
the *bottom tone* and add it above to arrive at the next inversion of the
chord. Sometimes the root G may be omitted, as shown below in the 3rd
inversion.

G7 (third inversion)

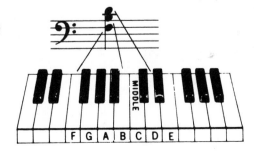

By utilizing these three chords—C, F, and G7—in certain chord positions, we can now play a given melody with both hands. The following melody will use these three chords in the positions we have covered.

First play each hand alone, then both hands together.

Beautiful Dreamer

Stephen Foster

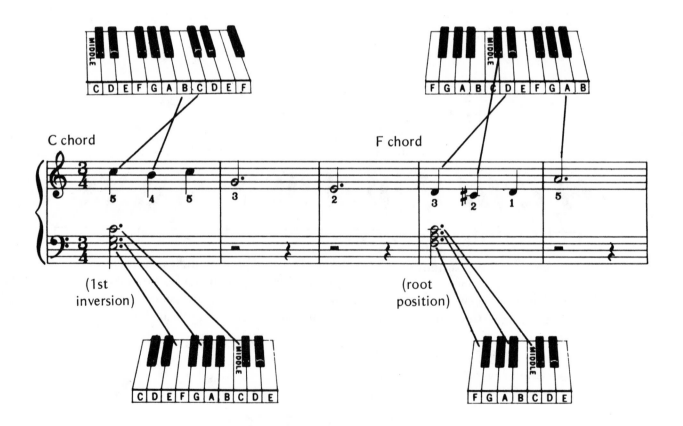

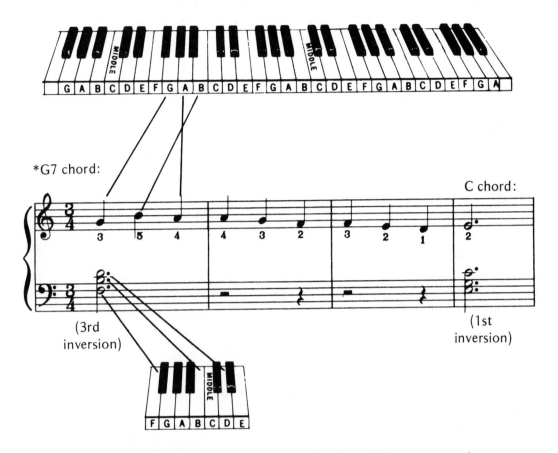

Now, without the aid of the preceding keyboard diagrams, continue to play the next nine bars.

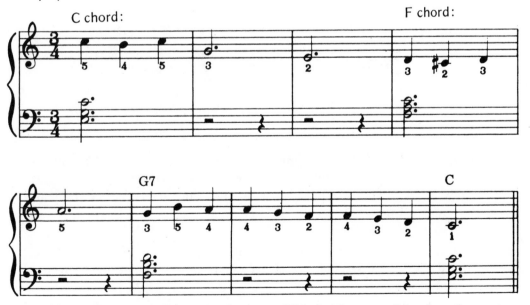

*The root is omitted here in the bass. This is often possible when the root note is in the melody.

With the chords we have covered we can now attempt to play the following songs in the Key of C:

You Tell Me Your Dream, I'll Tell You Mine

I Believe

Cool Water

Tennessee Waltz

Short'nin' Bread

Building Chords in the Key of F

Building chords on the Scale of F gives us the following:

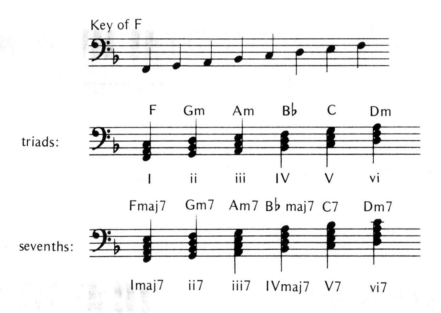

Notice, the above triads and sevenths are built in the same way as the chords in the key of C, and will retain the same qualities. However, we arrive at two new series of chord changes, as we are building on a new scale (F major scale in key of F).

If we were to build, for example, a ii chord on the G major scale, a ii chord on the E♭ major scale, and a ii chord on the A♭ major scale, we would have the following:

ii chord in G — A minor

ii chord in E♭ — F minor

ii chord in A♭ — B♭ minor.

Notice the quality of minor, a consistent factor in the above chords.

Let us now build two new chords in the Key of F. (see preceding page)

Selecting the IV chord (B♭) and the V7 chord (C7), we can illustrate their basic and inversion formations on the keyboard.

Play this Chord:

B♭ Chord:

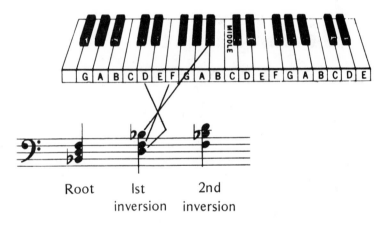

Root   lst   2nd
inversion inversion

C7 Chord:

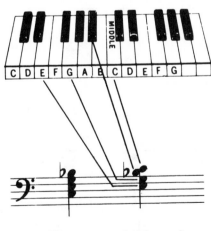
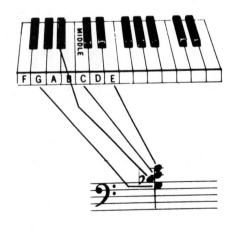

Root   1st inversion   2nd inversion

Using the F chord we previously covered and the two new chords, B♭ and C7, we can play *All Through the Night.*

Before playing this piece with both hands together, it is best to familiarize yourself with the song by:

1. playing the right hand alone;

2. playing the left hand alone while observing the position of the chords in relation to the keyboard;

3. noting that we are in the Key of F, with B♭ in the Key Signature; *i.e.* all notes on the B line in both clefs will be flatted or lowered one-half tone.

All Through the Night

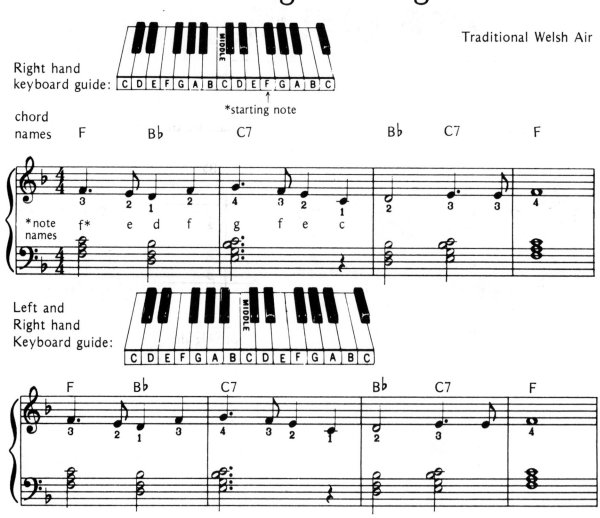

Traditional Welsh Air

————— *These four bars repeat note-for-note the first four bars.* —————

Continue playing *All Through the Night.* See if you can play the right hand
without the aid of the keyboard diagram.

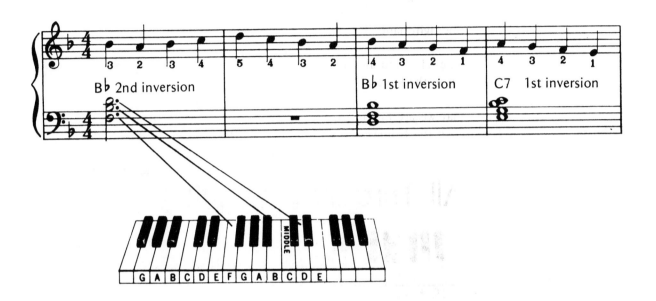

Now, concluding the song, play without the diagram for the left hand also.

With chords covered so far, we can now try playing the following songs
in the Key of F:

John Peel

Old Kentucky Home

Ricochet

CHAPTER 3

ROCK AND ROLL

Rock Chords are not any different from the chords we have studied so far—even in their construction. What determines the rock sound is the *way* the chords move and *how* they connect with another chord. True, while most so-called rock chords are simple in construction (many fall on the second inversion of major chords), the rock chord progression is influenced by the song, the group performing the song, and by other important elements.

Before illustrating chord progressions, it is important to study the right-hand chord inversions on the keyboard. So far we have confined ourselves to voicing the left hand. Here now are some inversions for the right hand.

Play the *C Chord:*   Now play the right hand inversions of C chord:

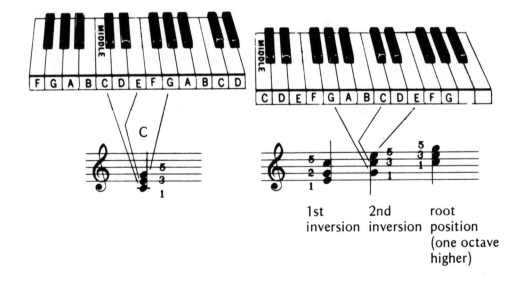

1st   2nd   root
inversion   inversion   position
                         (one octave
                         higher)

Play the *F Chord:*

Play inversions of F chord:

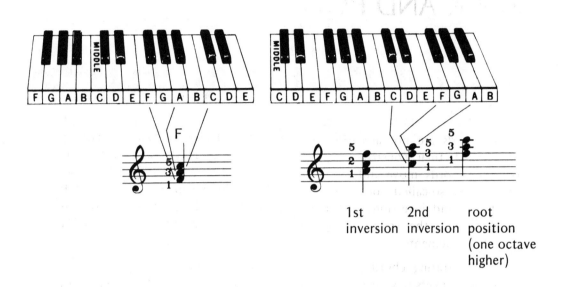

1st inversion   2nd inversion   root position (one octave higher)

Play the *G7 Chord:*

Play inversions of G7 chord:

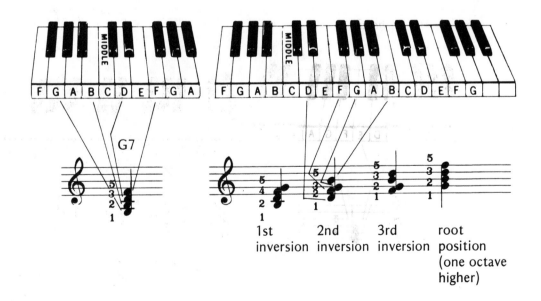

1st inversion   2nd inversion   3rd inversion   root position (one octave higher)

We will now study a few rock progressions based upon three chords of the C scale:

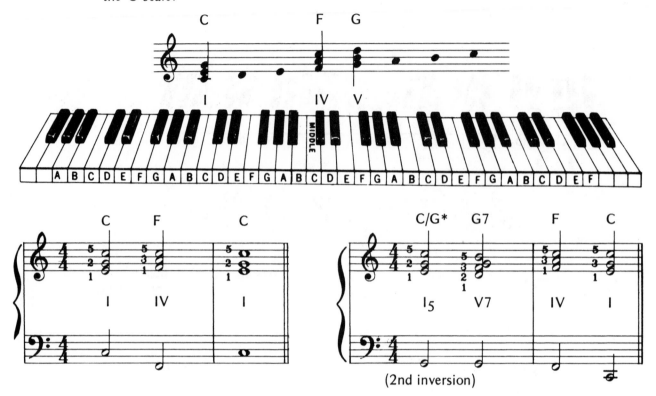

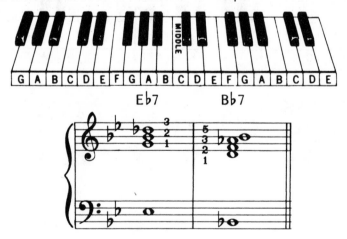

(2nd inversion)

An interesting chord progression, which has become somewhat of a favorite sound in rock music is the use of consecutive 7th chord progressions moving in intervals of four or two and a half steps.

*This is a C chord in the second inversion. It is noted C/G, because the bottom /G shows the inversion of the chord.

We will now construct two 7th chords, based on the B♭ scale, which we will play in a song exercise shortly.

Key of B♭:

B♭ C D E♭ F G A B♭

Important: You must remember that the key of B♭ has two flats, E♭ and B♭, and will carry through all the music written in this key.

We will now construct 7th chords in the key of B♭ by flatting the top tone.

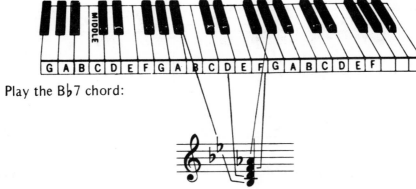

Play the B♭7 chord:

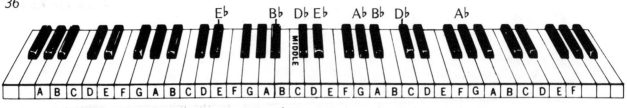

Now play the inversions of the B♭7 chord:

*root position   1st inversion   2nd inversion   3rd inversion   B♭7 chord
one octave higher

Play the E♭7 chord:  Refer to the keyboard above.
Don't forget the D♭!

Now play inversions of the E♭7 chord:

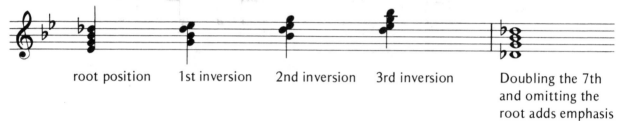

root position   1st inversion   2nd inversion   3rd inversion   Doubling the 7th
and omitting the
root adds emphasis
to the chord.

Play the following progression based on the two chords we just constructed:

*Remember when we play inversions, we take the bottom tone of the chord and place
it on top of the following chord.

Rock Rhythm

Rock rhythm is based upon an even four beats to the measure. In most rock songs, the tempo is a medium $\frac{4}{4}$.

This rhythm is then subdivided into more rhythmic patterns. A rock beat often heard that adapts itself to this variation is:

often this pattern becomes:

a still further division:

Many combinations of the above are possible as we shall soon see. Now practice the exercise on the following page. Either clap, beat time with your foot, or just hum the beat. Emphasize the accented tones marked thus:

Rock Rhythm Exercises

Repeat each exercise a few times. Set a medium rock tempo for all exercises:

Disco Rock:

Ballad style: Notice that the second and fourth beats come before the eighth note.

1 2 and 3 4 and   1 2 and 3   4

Left-Hand Rock Rhythm

We can now adapt the left hand to a rock rhythm. Let us select rhythm number 2:  Voicing this for the left hand gives us the following:

Notice, we do not use the entire Bb7 chord on the second and fourth beats. We use only the important harmonic tones. We must remember that what we are doing is using the left hand as a basic beat, somewhat in imitation of a drummer in a rock band laying down the 4's. A sparsely-voiced chord has more impact.

Now practice the Bb7 and Eb7 chords in rock rhythm for the left hand.

Important: Remember we are in the key of Bb. Bb has two flats, Eb and Bb and this will carry through for the entire line.

Medium Rock tempo:

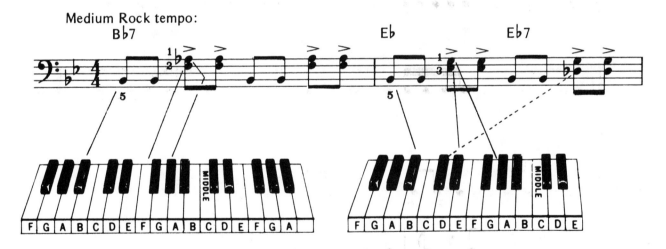

The next few pages contain an arrangement of a rock song I composed based upon two chord changes. If you practiced the chords and exercises in this chapter, you should be able to play it in medium tempo (after a little practice).

Rockin' Round the Apple

Music by Win Stormen

Beginners: It is best to practice the right and left hands separately. When you can play the melody in an even tempo with the right hand, *then* play both hands together.

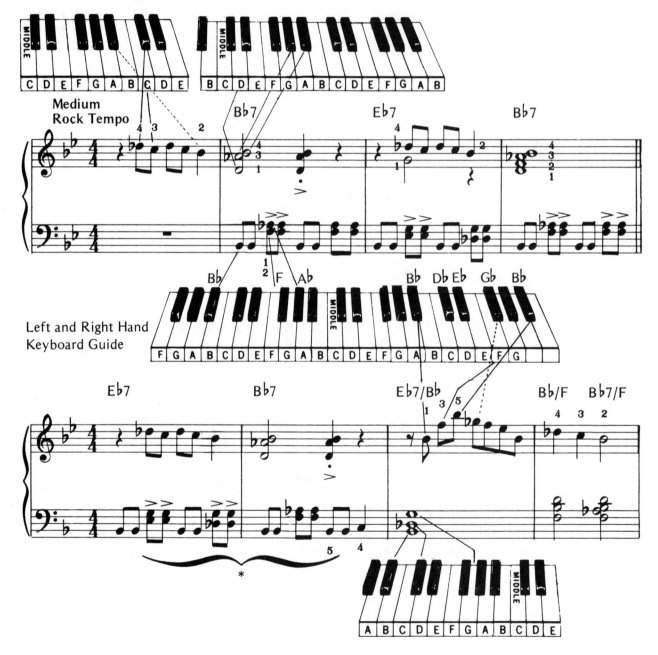

*These two bars are almost the same as the first two bars of the song. Try playing this, not using the keyboard guide.

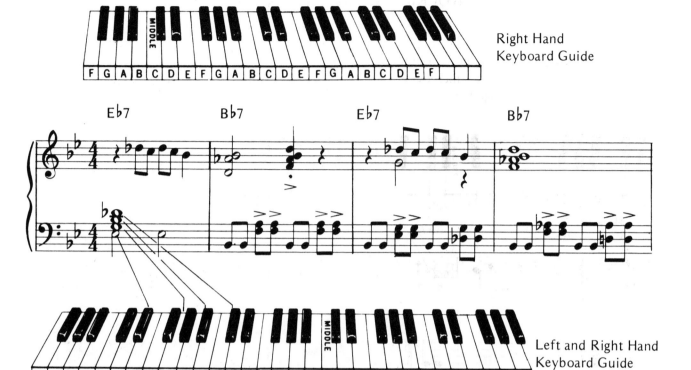

Right Hand
Keyboard Guide

Left and Right Hand
Keyboard Guide

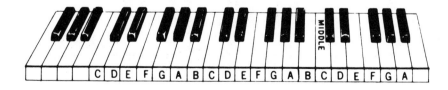

Left Hand
Keyboard Guide

CHAPTER 4
LET'S GO TO A DISCO

The lights flash. A pulsating, energizing beat catches you off guard. And, for a reason you can't explain, you feel good. The disco beat has suddenly become a part of you. At this moment the disco beat is the best friend you have, for it has slipped you into a new world. You are "there."

Where?

You don't know. You are just "there!" And you are more than glad to be there, for all your cares have faded away. Every thought has also disappeared...except one: Go with the beat. Another thought enters your mind as the crowd of vibrating bodies thickens: Find a partner and join the others, dancing through the flashing lights on the disco floor.

Let us hope you will not cast this book aside and run to the nearest disco! But if you have *never been*, I would say by all means, go. Words cannot completely describe the experience. Listening to disco music on the radio is not the same as being on the dance floor and moving to the beat. Remember, disco is primarily music for dancing rather than listening.

However, if you can't make it to a disco club, flip your FM radio dial to a *good* disco station. Better yet, buy a best-selling disco L.P. album.

Back to Reality!

The purpose of this book, of course, is self-instruction. When we learn by ourselves we must bring all our senses into focus, including *memory*. We must have some idea what a disco beat is like before we attempt to play it on the piano. Having heard disco on record, or having been to a disco club will remind us of the basics of this form of music. There are, of course, many disco rhythms. The basic pulse, in steady $\frac{4}{4}$ time, however, is always there.

The Basic Disco Beat

Playing disco on the piano can be very interesting when you have a good beat going in the left hand. The beat is in four quarter time and is almost a scintillating march beat. There are some slow and fast disco beats, but most are in medium tempo. There is some similarity to rock and roll, as the bass drum often accents the second and fourth beat:

Playing along with the bass drum are snares, Fender bass, Latin American percussion instruments, guitar, synthesizers, and electric or amplified acoustic piano. The combined sound soon evolves into one singular sensation that dancers eagerly respond to.

A very important part of the disco beat is a syncopated, rhythmic phrase that occurs throughout a disco arrangement. It is often heard in the introduction by the electric guitar or Fender bass. Slowly, the arrangement builds over this with strings coming in, then the melody with voices or other instruments. It is this off beat, very catchy phrase that we shall try to capture on the piano. Best of all, we will try to make up our own. I have written out some practice phrases in subsequent pages.

The next page illustrates disco rhythms for the left hand. It is important to practice this before playing a disco song. It is also a good idea to hum or clap the rhythms before playing it on the piano. Tap your foot to the rhythm as you go along. You might think of your foot as the bass drum effect. Keep it going at a steady $\left(\frac{4}{4}\ \downarrow\ \downarrow\ \downarrow\ \downarrow \right)$ beat as you practice the rhythms below.

Left Hand Disco Rhythms

Practice each exercise three times. When you can play each one smoothly, accenting where indicated, you will know you have mastered these exercises.

Disco Rhythm Exercises (continued)

7.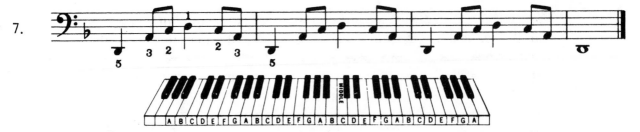

Building Chords in F Major (right hand)

We have previously constructed chords on the major scales for the left hand. This chapter will emphasize the right hand.

Following is the scale of F major:

Major and minor chords:

Dominant seventh, Major and Minor 7th chords:

Remember: We simply add notes on consecutive lines and spaces to build our chords.

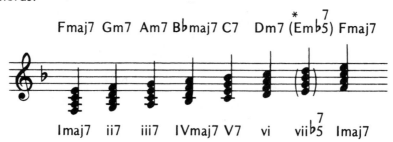

*Diminished chords and flatted 5th chords are studied separately in later chapters.

Ninth chords are constructed in a manner similar to the 7th and major chords. We add a consecutive line or space over the top 7th tone of the scale:

Notice, the quality of the chord remains the same. We simply change the 7th chord to a ninth chord. This is how songs are notated in popular sheet music. As it is difficult to play the right hand as notated above, we must voice the right hand by leaving out certain tones. The root can be omitted in the right hand if it is played in the left hand.

The fifth sometimes may be omitted:

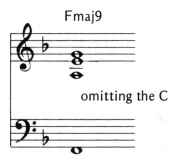

omitting the C

Chord Exercises

It is important to practice the following exercises. They will prepare you to play the disco song at the end of this chapter.

Play F major chord root and inversions with right hand:

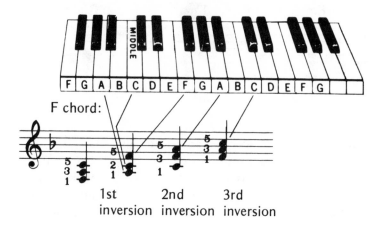

Remember: When we form inversions we take the bottom tone and place it on top of the chord.

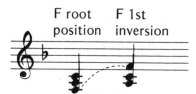

Play Fmaj7 both positions as indicated.

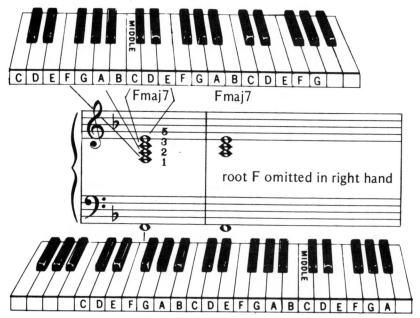

Play Fmaj9 chord.   Note the difference in sound of the two voicings of this chord.

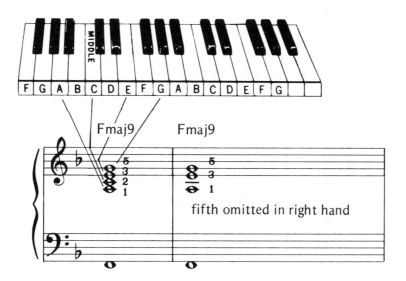

Play all inversions of the C7 chord.   Remember when you play an inversion of a C7 chord, you take the bottom tone of the preceding C7 chord, and you place it above the top note of chord.

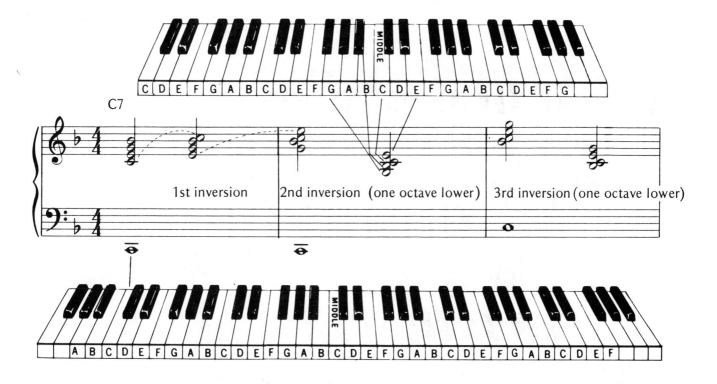

Minor Chords

The minor chords we will now practice are:

Play the *G Minor Chord* in root position and inversions:

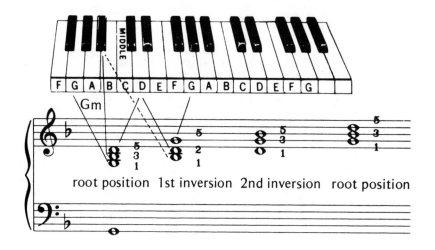

root position   1st inversion   2nd inversion   root position

Play the *A Minor Chord* in root position and inversions:

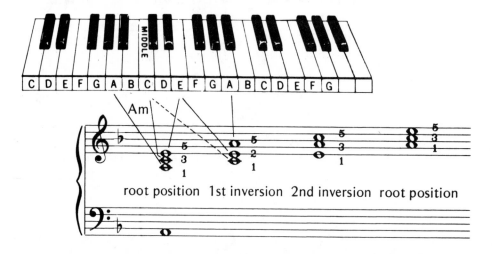

root position   1st inversion   2nd inversion   root position

D Minor Chord: Play right hand alone in root and inversions (see next page):

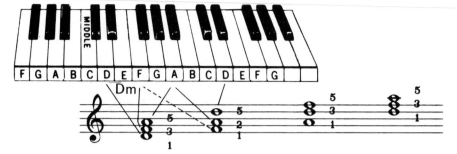

root position 1st inversion 2nd inversion root position

Changing the Minor Chord to Major

To change a minor chord to major, raise the third note of the chord one-half step:

We will encounter the A7 chord in a song on the following pages. It is built upon the A chord above, to which a tone is added one and a half steps above the third note of the chord:

A + 7th tone=A7

A Briefing Before Playing Disco Song

You are now ready to play a disco song. The material in this chapter has covered all chords and inversions used in the song. Practice will facilitate finding the chord positions on the piano, when they suddenly appear in in the sheet music. Do not expect to play this song perfectly in the first session. Beginners should take a section at a time.

A good idea is to learn the basic left hand disco rhythm first. When you have mastered this, play the right hand separately, *then*, play both hands together.

Let's Go To A Disco

Words and Music by Win Stormen

Medium disco tempo

(A repeat of 1st bar)   (repeat of 1st bar)

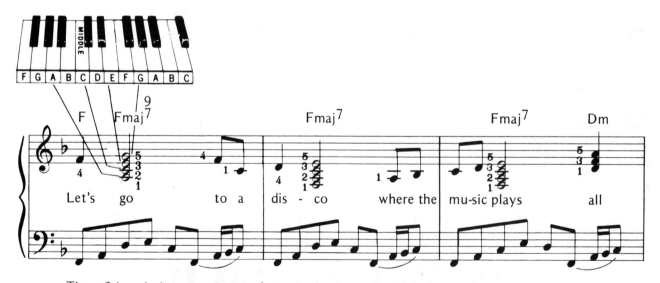

F   Fmaj⁷⁹   Fmaj⁷   Fmaj⁷   Dm

Let's go   to a   dis - co   where the mu-sic plays   all

These 3 bars in bass repeat note for note the above first 3 bars.

night. _____ Where the lights flash, and the vibes flow and sud-den-ly sud-den - ly ev-'ry-thing's all right. _____ With light wine, in the night time, we'll get it all to - geth - er, _____ rain or snow, sleet or hail,

53

who's gon-na talk a-bout the weath-er?

When I'm with my

ba - by, noth-ing else mat-ters to me. _____ The

band flies a-way to the near-est star, and fif-ty dancin' feet

do the boogie woogie in a mi - nor key.

Disco beat solo

disco break —

ad libitum

R. H.

slowly, in rhythm:

L.H.

A tempo, (faster)

Repeat three times (Play one octave higher the third time)

It's

*If this break is too difficult, omit it and proceed to the glissando.

58

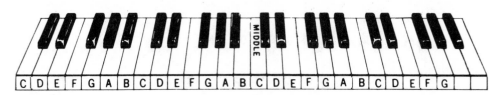

CHAPTER 5
SPANNING THE OCTAVE

If a saxophonist in an orchestra played the chorus of a song many times over, after a while the music would sound dull and ineffective. Add, however, two or three saxophones, and perhaps part of the brass section to fill in the harmony, and the music takes on more color and interest.

Playing through a song using only one finger of the right hand would soon take on the monotonous tone of the lone saxophonist. Just as the various instruments of the orchestra supply the missing harmony tones to fill out a song, the second, third, and fourth fingers of the right hand accomplish the same purpose for the piano. Before illustrating this, we should first learn to "double the melody line" by playing the melody in *octaves*.

Instead of playing the melody with only one finger of the right hand, we double the melody an octave higher with the fifth finger. (Later, we will see how to fill in the harmony by using the second, third, and fourth fingers.)

By testing a few notes, playing octaves, we observe the following:

1. We play the lower melody tone with the first finger of the right hand.
2. We play the top melody tone with the fifth finger of the right hand.
3. We keep the wrist parallel to the fingers.
4. We get a hollow sound upon striking the following tones:

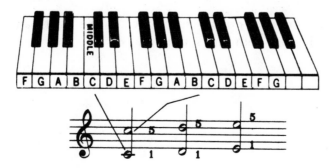

Now play the following scales as a preparatory exercise for spanning the octave:

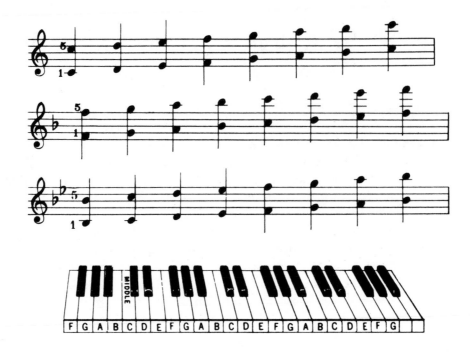

To accustom the right hand to the swing of popular music, play the following rhythms:

Try the following excerpt playing octaves in the right hand. Play each hand separately, then both hands together.

The Band Played On

Charles B. Ward

The next chapter will illustrate octaves with the swing bass.

CHAPTER 6

LEFT HAND RHYTHMS

Beginners: If you find this chapter a little too difficult, please proceed to the next one.

To color a popular song and make it swing rhythmically, we can add several different bass rhythms. Let us start with the simplest rhythm, often called stride piano when played in fast tempos:

Stride piano is often referred to as a swing bass and can be used for popular songs in cut time (₵) for ballads, swing, novelty and blues songs.

As we begin to learn the swing bass, let us remember to accent the second and fourth beats slightly. When we learn to play songs we can sometimes vary the accent according to the tempo and mood of a particular song. Songs that move very fast will have an even beat in swing bass, without any accent. Or, pianists may add their own touch and accent a certain beat according to a particular whim.

Use the root and fifth of a chord on the first and third beats and keep the chords within this range on the second and fourth beats:

The swing bass changes with the chord change:

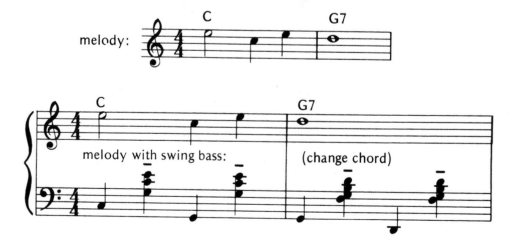

Beginning to Play Stride Piano

Practice the following left-hand rhythmic chord positions placing a slight accent on the second and fourth beats. Try to achieve an even swing to the rhythm. Use a metronome if necessary.

Left Hand
Keyboard Guide

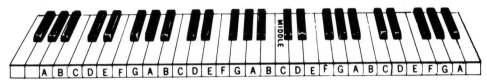

Ex. 1 Major Chord Exercise

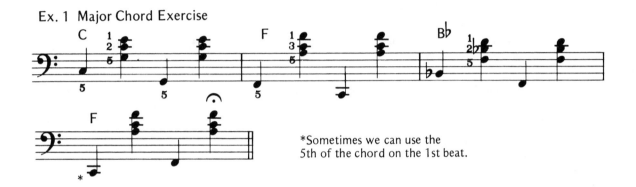

*Sometimes we can use the
5th of the chord on the 1st beat.

Ex. 2 Minor Chord Exercise

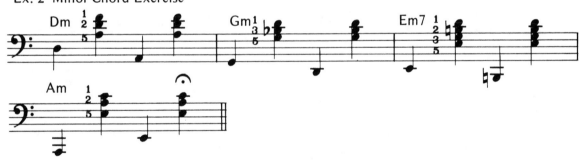

Ex. 3 This is an exercise of the Dominant 7th resolving to a Major 7th chord.

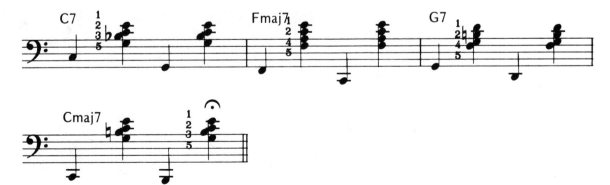

Notice that we classified the chords on the preceding page as

| Major | Minor | Minor 7th | Major 7th | Dominant 7th |

A few observations on sound:

The *major* chord is neutral and cheerful in contrast with the minor chord whose sound is somber and somewhat mysterious.

The *minor* 7th chord has a less somber quality than the minor chord, with a softer sound.

The *dominant* 7th chord has a strong sound, whereas the *major* 7th has a more sentimental quality.

Left-Hand Swing Bass Exercises

The following exercises will prepare you to play the song on the next page. Pause after each chord change. Be aware of the contrast in quality of each chord.

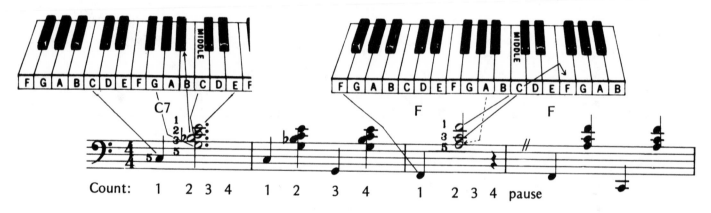

Count: 1   2 3 4   1   2   3   4   1   2 3 4 pause

The Fm chord below is in the same position as the preceding chord, with an A♭ added.

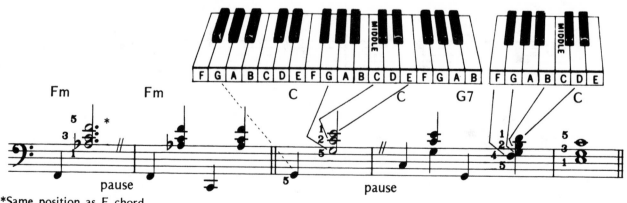

*Same position as F chord
with a lowered third (a♭).

Repeat the next four bars a few times:

You Fly the Blues Away

Music by Win Stormen

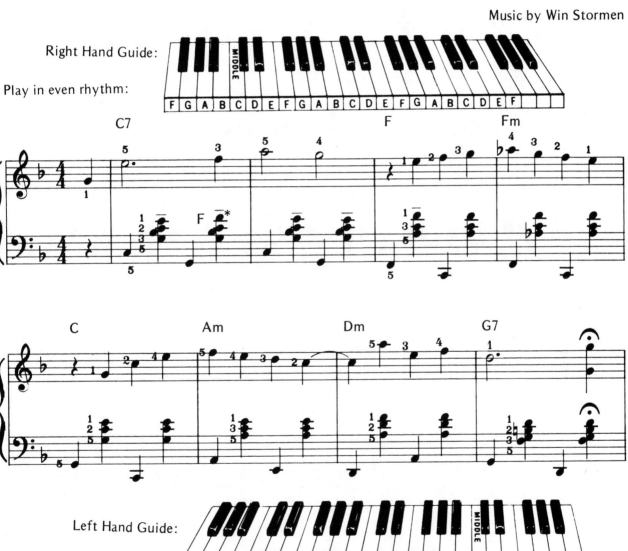

Top note was changed to an F for a more pleasing sound. These adjustments sometimes are made in swing bass.

The left and right hands are repeated exactly as before, except that now the right hand plays octaves.

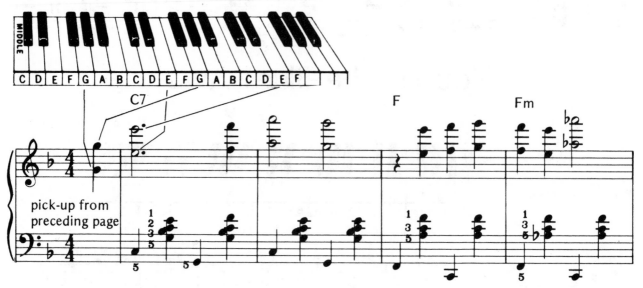

Left and Right Hand Guide:

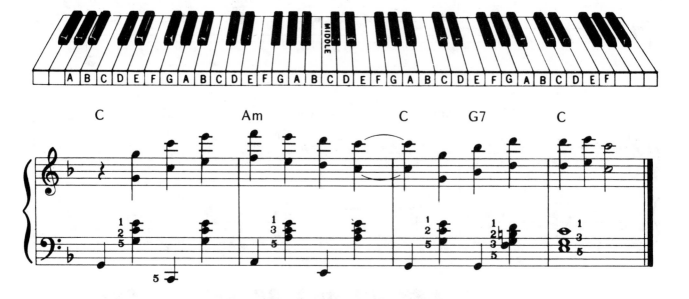

Left Hand Guide:

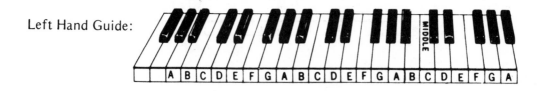

CHAPTER 7
STUDIES IN SYNCOPATION

One of the elements contributing to the success of a popular song is the use of offbeat or syncopated rhythms which often underlie the drive or beat in popular music. Another is a song's interpretation by different vocalists, who often change rhythmic content to fit their individual styles.

Note that the study of various syncopated patterns constitutes added practice for the right hand. Following is one of the most frequently found syncopated patterns with an explanation of how it is counted.

In many cases, ♪. 𝄐 is substituted for ♪ ♪ and is written 𝅘𝅥𝅮 𝄐 in piano arrangements.

In counting one full beat for the syncopated pattern, ♪. 𝄐, we observe that the first note is accented and the second note, coming in at the end of the beat, is unaccented.

Counting this pattern in strict metered time, we give the first note, ♪., three-quarters of a beat and the second note, 𝄐, one-quarter of a beat. The following examples illustrate how ♪. 𝄐 rhythm is metered compared to the ♪♪ rhythm.

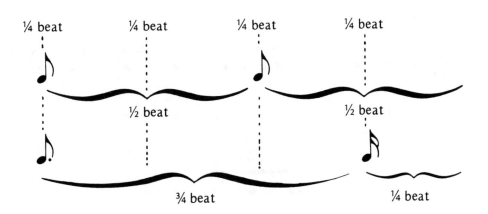

¼ beat   ¼ beat   ¼ beat   ¼ beat

½ beat   ½ beat

¾ beat   ¼ beat

In ♪♪ rhythm we divide the beat exactly in half and count "one" for the first half of the beat, ♪, then "and" for the second half of the beat, ♪. In counting out the rhythm ♪. ♪, we count "one and" for the first note (exactly as in the rhythm ♪♪). The second note, ♪, is not counted, but played fast to lead into the next beat. The diagram below illustrates how to count these rhythms.

Hum and count the following rhythmic exercises:

Another rhythm often found in popular music is the Triplet:

A slight accent is given to the first note of the triplet which is played or sung by dividing it into three equal parts, with each note receiving one-third of a beat.

Hum and count the following rhythmic exercises:

With only the aid of the keyboard diagram, play the song on the next page illustrating the Triplet.

With only the aid of the keyboard diagram below, play the following song illustrating the Triplet.

Down in the Valley

Traditional Song

Tied Notes

Another syncopated or offbeat device is the *tied note*. Only the first note of tied notes is sounded. The other note is sustained for its corresponding time value.

Two or more notes can be tied:

In humming and counting out the following rhythms, hum the sustained tied notes, keeping the meter in mind.

You Tell Me Your Dreams, I'll Tell You Mine

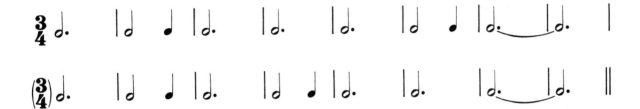

Rock and Roll, Rhythm and Blues

This chapter has primarily dealt with syncopation. Most of the music we hear today, such as *Rock and Roll, Rhythm and Blues,* employs syncopation.

Hum the following rock and roll rhythms and accent the second and fourth beats. Notice the difference between the rock beat of the fifties and today's beat.

Rock beat of the fifties:

Today's sound:

Hum the following Rhythm and Blues beat. Compare it to the Rock and Roll beat.

This same rhythm can also have an accent on the second and fourth beats.

Hum the following rhythm in the same Rhythm and Blues meter above, but don't forget to put in the accents.

CHAPTER 8
THE AUGMENTED CHORD

The *Augmented Chord* in popular music has a most unusual sound and has been given such names as "the nostalgic chord," "the haunted chord," and "the cool chord." As you play it other names may come to you.

The Augmented Chord resembles a Major Chord, with one exception. It is formed by raising the fifth tone (third note) of the major triad by one-half step:

The following examples show how augmented chords are formed in a few other keys. A complete list of augmented chords appears in The Chord Index.

With the aid of the keyboard diagram practice a few chords for the left hand.

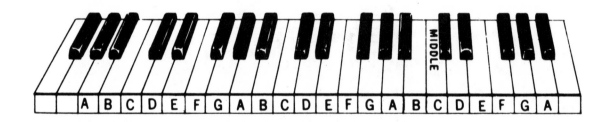

In the next chapter we will see how the *augmented chord* is used in a popular song.

CHAPTER 9

DIMINISHED 7th AND MINOR CHORDS

The *diminished 7th chord* is an interesting one and can be spelled in many ways; its sound, however, remains the same.

Actually, there are only three possible constructions of diminished 7th chords. The fact that it is used in several keys accounts for its various spellings.

Let us examine the three different diminished 7th chords used in popular music and see how they are constructed.

Constructing Diminished 7th Chords

Theoretically, we can assemble *diminished 7th chords* by the natural laws of harmony. However, to simplify the learning process, and to be able to recognize and play diminished 7th chords, we will write them in the easiest manner.

To form the
$$\begin{cases} \text{E dim. 7*} \\ \text{C}\sharp \text{ dim. 7} \\ \text{G dim. 7} \\ \text{B}\flat \text{ dim. 7} \end{cases}$$

Form a C7 chord:

C7

Then raise the root of the C7: (see next page)

*The name of the diminished 7th chord can be taken from any one of the four notes in the chord.

C⁷ chord with raised root c♯.

This gives us C♯ dim. 7, E dim. 7, G dim. 7, or B♭ dim. 7.

To form the
{
D dim. 7
F dim. 7
A♭ dim. 7
B dim. 7
}

Form a G7 chord:

G7

Then raise the root:

This gives us D dim. 7, F dim. 7, A♭ dim. 7 (G♯dim.7), or B dim. 7.

To form the
{
E♭ dim. 7
F♯ dim. 7
A dim. 7
C dim. 7
}

Form an F7 chord:

F7

Then raise the root:

This gives us F♯ dim. 7, A dim. 7, C dim. 7, E♭ dim. 7.

Notice the left-hand positions of Dim. 7 chords below.
Using the simple swing bass, we have:

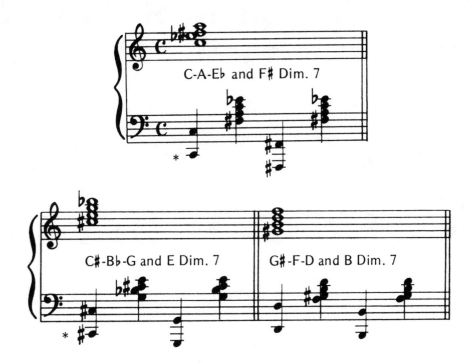

Minor Chords

Minor chords are somber in sound quality. They are formed by lowering or flatting the third of a major chord.

Practice these chords with your left hand:

*Bottom tone optional

By using the chords we have constructed, we can play the following melody. Play each hand separately, then both together.

After The Ball

Music by C. K. Harris

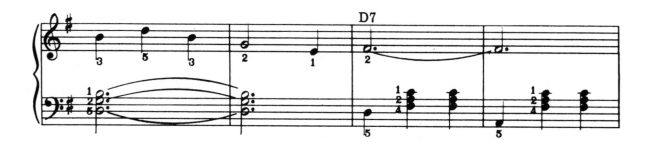

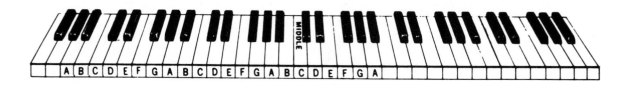

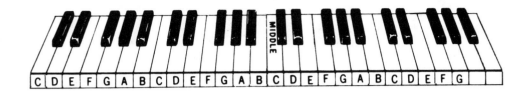

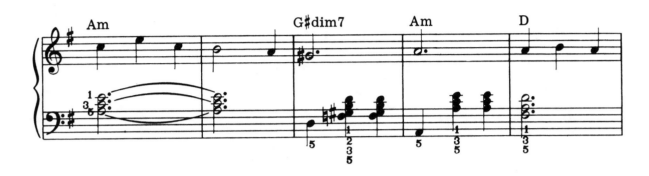

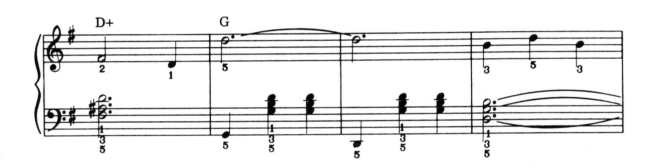

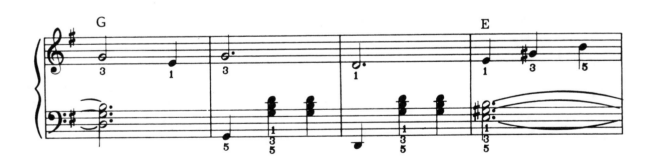

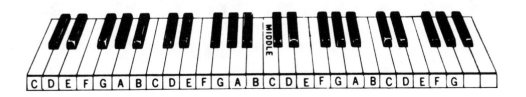

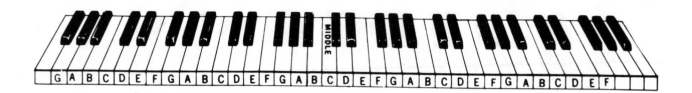

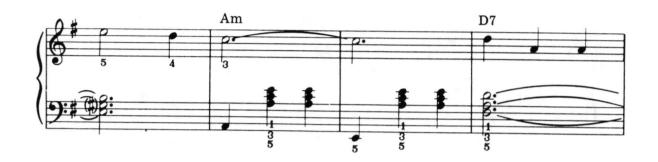

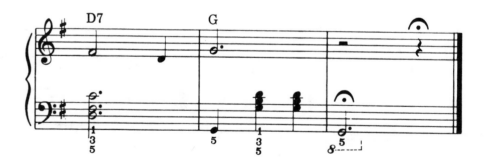

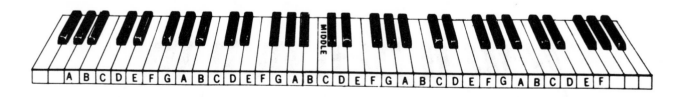

CHAPTER 10
A LITTLE THEORY

This chapter may be used to advantage by students who have had some previous experience in reading music. Therefore, beginners should not become discouraged if a few of the examples illustrated seem too difficult. Just go on to Chapter 11.

Knowing *why* certain chords follow other chords helps us learn *how* to play the piano. Many who have studied harmony are able to play popular piano without the aid of an instructor. After you have mastered the theory covered so far and practiced its application, you will find yourself unconsciously playing certain breaks or chords to fill in melodies or color a popular song.

Let us briefly review the formation of chords before taking up new chords.

Review of Chord Formation

The chords we have studied so far are built on the tones of the scale. To build Diatonic Chords, first select a major scale.

C major scale:

To the notes on lines, add two notes on consecutive lines above and to the notes in spaces, add two notes in consecutive spaces above to form triads.

I   ii   iii   IV   V   vi   (viiº)

Each triad has a numeral beneath. The numerals indicate the kind or quality of chord they represent.

I, IV, and V are major chords.

ii, iii, and vi are minor chords.

vii° is a diminished chord. As mentioned before, it is rarely used in popular music. However, when we add a 7th to the diminished chord it becomes a diminished 7th and is found quite often in popular sheet music.

Substituting chord letter names for the symbols gives us:

C   Dm   Em   F   G   Am   (B°)*

Using the chord letter names for the first six chords, we have:

C   Dm   Em   F   G   Am

In popular sheet music, chords are written above the melody line.

Formation of 7th Chords

To form *7th chords,* add one note on the next line above the triads and one note in the next space above the triads. Symbols and chord letter names are as follows:

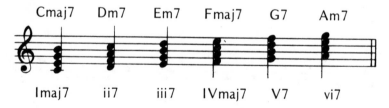

Cmaj7   Dm7   Em7   Fmaj7   G7   Am7

Imaj7   ii7   iii7   IVmaj7   V7   vi7

Inversions may be used with any triad or 7th chords.

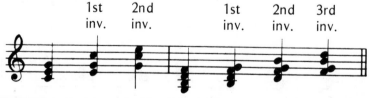

1st   2nd   1st   2nd   3rd
inv.   inv.   inv.   inv.   inv.

*B° the diminished chord is used with a 7th added and is notated B dim. 7 (See Chapter 9 on Diminished Chords.)

Formation of 9th Chords

To form *9th chords,* add one note on the line and one note in the space above the sevenths. Note that the iii—9 chord is lowered or flatted because of the way major scales are formed. In diatonic harmony, the iii—9 chord is the *only* minor chord. (See further Chapter 12.)

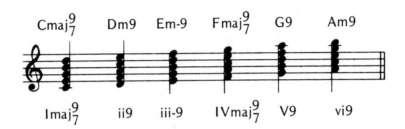

The Added Sixth

A sixth may be added to any major or minor triad to produce a more modern sound.

The *added sixth* is formed by adding one whole step to the fifth, or last tone, of a triad.

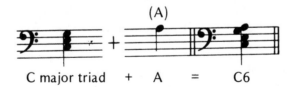

C major triad + A = C6

Play over the following chords and listen to the sound of the *added sixth:*

Dm6   F6   E♭6   D♭6   C6

Having seen how chords are constructed, let us now observe how they progress or "move" in popular music.

Diatonic and Chromatic Chords

Chords may be either diatonic or chromatic. Diatonic chords are built upon tones of the major scales. Chromatic chords are altered diatonic chords and are discussed later.

Diatonic Chord Progression

Analyze the Diatonic Progressions on the charts below to see how they are used. The first column under Diatonic Progressions indicates the chord you may start with in harmonizing a melody. The "Usual Progression" column indicates the chord that *usually* follows the opening chord. The "1st Alternate" column includes chords that *sometimes* follow the opening chord. The "2nd Alternate" column includes chords that *least often* follow the opening chord.

Example: Starting with the vi chord we have this pattern:

    vi   ii   V   I   IV   V   I

vi usually is followed by ii; ii is usually followed by V; V is usually followed by I, etc. In the key of C, the chord progression for the above symbols is:

    Am   Dm   G   C   F   G   C

In harmonizing melodies, the chords to be chosen will vary, however, with the melody. In most cases the "Usual Progression" column is used in choosing the chord to follow. Should this conflict with the melody, the alternate columns can be used.

All progression goes toward any one chord within a box. For example, IV or V7 or vi, etc., is a usual progression of the I chord. (See "Usual Progression" column, first line.*)

Diatonic Progressions

	Usual Progression	*1st Alternate*	*2nd Alternate*
I	IV, V7, V vi, vi7	ii, ii7	iii, iii7
Imaj7	IV, vi vi7	I, V V7	ii, ii7 iii, iii7
ii ii7	V, V7	iii, iii7	I, IV
iii, iii7	vi, vi7	ii, ii7, IV	V, V7
IV	V, V7, I	ii, ii7	iii
IVmaj7	ii7, ii	I	—
V, V7	I, vi vi7	IV, ii ii7	iii, iii7
vi, vi7	ii, ii7	iii, iii7 IV, V7	I

The substitution of chord letter names for symbols in the key of C is illustrated in the following chart:

Key of C

	Usual Progression	*1st Alternate*	*2nd Alternate*
C	F, G7, G Am, Am7	Dm, Dm7	Em, Em7
Cmaj7	F, Am, Am7	C, G, G7	Dm, Dm7, Em Em7
Dm Dm7	G, G7	Em, Em7	C, F
Em Em7	Am, Am7	Dm, Dm7, F	G, G7
F	G, G7, C	Dm, Dm7	Em
Fmaj7	Dm7, Dm	C	—
G, G7	C, Am, Am7	F, Dm, Dm7	Em, Em7
Am, Am7	Dm, Dm7	Em, Em7, F, G7	C

By playing the progressions illustrated in the following examples, we can associate the sound of each chord with the chord letter and symbol names.

Note that the left hand in the following examples falls within this range:

These chord voicings are designed for two purposes:

1. To synchronize the left hand to popular music.
2. For general ear training and chord association.

DIATONIC USUAL PROGRESSIONS

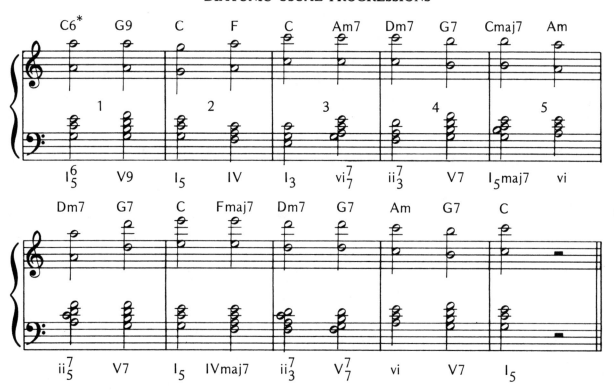

Beginners: If these examples prove too difficult to play, go on to *Merry Widow Waltz,* page 88.

The following are the *diatonic usual progressions* in the key of F. These should be played over, associating the chord letter name with the chord symbol name.

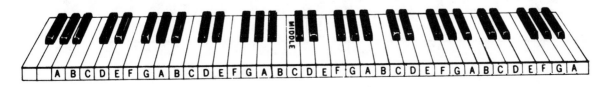

Below is an example of the I, V7, I chord progression in the key of F.

Merry Widow Waltz

Music by Franz Lehar

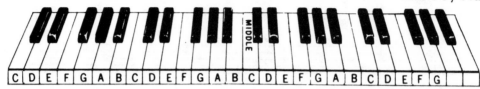

Notice that the chords are repeated over a few bars. These chords are strong basic progressions and are used frequently for easier melodies.

Here is another I, V7, I chord progression in the key of C.

Skater's Waltz

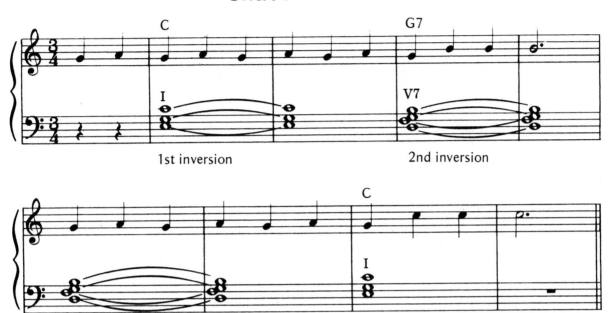

1st inversion   2nd inversion

Below is an example of a ii7, V7, I chord progression, most often used at the end of a musical phrase or song.

Polovetzian Dance

Music by Alexander Borodin

The Circle of Fifths

Another type of progression often used in popular music is known as the *Circle of Fifths*. It allows the use of three or more consecutive progressions in fifths to take us out of the tonality of the original key. The Circle of Fifths is thus a separate chord progression system and is not classified within the diatonic, chromatic, or other divisions of harmony.

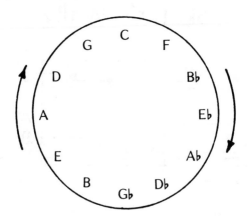

Each letter within the circle represents a triad on which seventh and ninth chords may be built. Starting on any triad and moving clockwise, the chords thus progress in fifths. It is sometimes possible to progress consecutively through six chords. For example:

C7   F7   B♭9   E♭9   A♭7   D♭7   etc.

The following illustrates the Circle of Fifths on the keyboard:

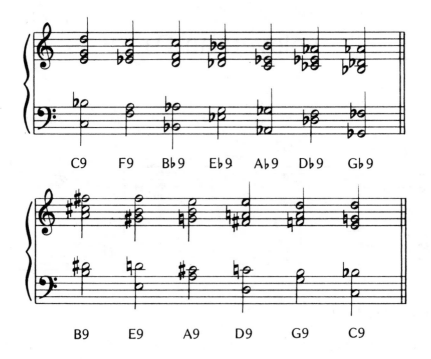

CHAPTER 11
JAZZ—HOT AND COOL

A good jazz man plays by instinct. He plays in his *own* style. Through the years, individual styles of playing have been influenced by the different eras in the gradual evolution of jazz. Scott Joplin and Jelly Roll Morton were the great jazz men of the early 1900's; Oscar Peterson, Herbie Hancock and Keith Jarret are piano jazz men of today.

Many authorities claim that jazz, in its pure form, is all improvisation with harmonic restriction in which the melody line ceases to be heard as a melody. Instead, the performer interprets the melody as he hears it. In many cases, in his interpretation, the melody line may be obscured, if not lost. Others prefer to divide jazz into various categories, or schools. Starting from the earliest forms to the present, these are basically Ragtime, Dixieland, Swing, Be-Bop, (Modern Jazz) and Fusion.

Ragtime, one of the earliest forms of jazz, was a syncopated style used by early pioneer pianists, such as Scott Joplin and J. E. Lamb. This music is played exactly as it is written. Somewhat later, Jelly Roll Morton started improvising on the melody line and became one of the earliest and best improvisors of his era. Jelly Roll Morton also claims that he "invented" jazz; the sign, "World's Greatest Hot Tune Writer and Inventor of Jazz" often appeared on his piano.

Dixieland, a style that at first did not include the piano, involved ensemble voicing for five or six instruments, such as the cornet, trombone, drums, bass, and banjo. Today with the piano added, Dixieland is as popular as it was from the early 1900's onward, and is performed by small groups throughout the country.

Swing, which became popular just before World War II, is still played today. Glenn Miller, Artie Shaw, Benny Goodman, and Charlie Barnett led some of the great bands of that era. Each band had its own unique arrangements by which it could be identified. Today, there are swing bands, like Woody Herman's, that still tour the U.S.A. and many college and high school bands play the arrangements of the 1940's and 1950's.

Be-Bop was the first name, or one of the first names, given to the new style of jazz played after World War II. Today we call this style, which has gone through considerable development, modern jazz. Most of the smaller groups, consisting of from three to six members, mostly play modern jazz. The piano is, of course, the backbone of the group along with the rhythm section of bass and drums and occasionally the guitar. Other instruments are the sax, trumpet and flute. Miles Davis, Dizzie Gillespie, Thelonious Monk, Oscar Peterson were the great pioneers of this jazz form and each one developed it further in his own style.

Let us now return to a discussion of an early style of jazz, the Blues, that was quite popular when it first appeared in the 1900's, and is still played today by every conceivable jazz ensemble.

The Blues Progression

The blues progression is simple in structure and many times forms the complete chord pattern of a popular song chorus. In many choruses the blues pattern is repeated two or three times (with different lyrics for each chorus). The blues progression is constructed over the following basic chords:

I *I7 IV I V7 I

The above progression, sustained over 12 bars, makes up one complete chorus of a blues song. For each chord in succession:

I extends thru 3 bars.
I7 ” ” 1 bar.
IV ” ” 2 bars.
I ” ” 2 bars.
V7 ” ” 2 bars.
I ” ” 2 bars.

*Sometimes in the blues pattern, I7 is notated Ib7.

In the key of C, then, the melody is constructed over the following chords:

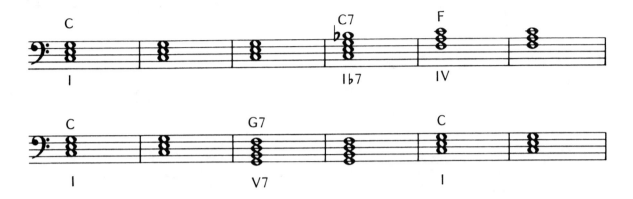

In the key of F, the blues progression is:

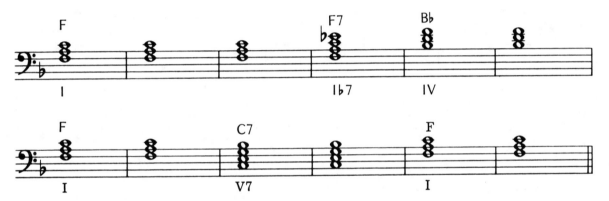

The left-hand bass in a blues progression can be played as octaves, as shown in Example 1, on the next page, and is sometimes called *boogie woogie.*

Examples 2 and 3 illustrate the left hand *boogie woogie* bass in a more concentrated rhythm. Observe the fingering.

Boogie Woogie:

Any song having a blues progression for either the whole or a part of the song can use either of the preceding basses for the left hand.

Example 3 on the next page illustrates a *honky tonk* rhythm that was characteristic of early blues piano playing.

Honky tonk boogie:

Here is an easy *boogie woogie* bass. It is also sometimes used for Western songs to give a riding effect.

The following song illustrates a Blues Progression written by W. C. Handy, a foremost composer of Blues.

St. Louis Blues
Words and Music by W. C. Handy

Beginners: Use top melody only, if right hand is too difficult.

Modern Jazz

An interesting modern jazz piano style is locked hand playing. It uses the right and left hands playing in locked hand positions. Here the left hand plays the melody as a single note together with the right hand. The right hand plays the melody, filling in with the first, second, third, and fourth fingers.

Locked Hand Style

This style can be substituted for the left hand swing bass (Chapter 6, pages 62—63).

Before attempting to learn this style, however, the standard styles previously illustrated should be mastered.

Modern Jazz Piano as Compared to Popular Piano

As beginners of popular piano study, we should be aware that the musicians who play modern jazz piano are playing in the contemporary style of today. Of course as beginners you cannot hope to play like professionals. But what you can do, is learn to appreciate the modern style. An understanding of this style might also encourage you to take up the study of this fascinating style of playing. And now a little analysis of modern jazz piano.

The Basic Beat

The basic beat in modern jazz is derived from the steady cymbal beat of the drummer in a small combo. Instead of the accents on the first and third beats, or second and fourth beats from the foot pedal, a steady 4-beat rhythm is produced by the cymbals in four quarter time and is notated as follows:

The Rhythms of Modern Jazz

The rhythms in modern jazz can be divided into background rhythms and melody line rhythms. Background rhythms played by the drummer in the small combo are quite complex at times; at other times they are a simple, steady four solid beats to the bar.

The melody line, played solo and at one time syncopated, is today played in smooth legato style. Note the difference in the following example:

To help you get the feel of modern jazz, here is an interesting experiment: Try tapping your foot to the following rhythm. Do not accent any portions of the beat. Keep it steady.

This is the basic rhythm of modern jazz.

Now try humming or playing this rhythm on the piano with the left hand only as follows:

Notice that the left hand is marked

This means you are to play the left hand as a bass would play the bass. Do not accent it hard; at the same time give it a definite thump. Also notice a dot below the note. A dot in this position indicates that the note is played as a staccato; that is after playing the note lightly, pick your hand up almost immediately upon hitting the note.

The added accent ( ) means to give it a definite beat, but at the same time do not accent it. To be really accurate, try listening to the bass of any modern jazz group.

Modern Jazz Chords

Although it is impossible for beginners to play the harmonies a jazz pianist in a group plays, it is possible, to hear the sound immediately of one chord played in the modern jazz idiom.

We can also compare this sound with the chord from which it was derived. Let us take the simple Dm7 chord. Play the following chord with the right hand.

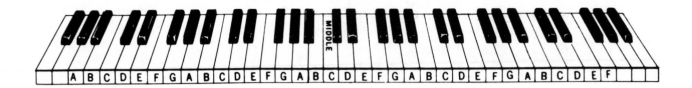

Now, let us add a G minor 7th chord below this. The trend today in playing modern chords is to add another chord to the one you are playing and play them both together.

As the G minor 7th chord consists of two tones similar to that of the Dm7 chord, we will only add two tones as follows for the left hand. Play with both hands.

Now just to give it an ultra modern effect, let us flat the 5th tone of the chord which is D flat. Now play this chord:

This is a full voicing, a somewhat lush effect. A modern jazz voicing of this is:

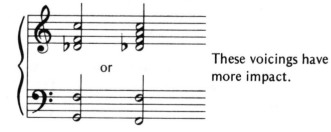

These voicings have more impact.

The Cool Sounds of Modern Jazz

The alto saxophonist wails far into the night. He plays chorus after chorus, song after song, of the old standards. Sometimes you hear the melody line. You recognize it as a few bars from a standard tune. Suddenly it is lost in a swinging arrangement of improvised tones. The notes are faster, closer together, and swinging. The melody line is lost. In its place is the musician's conception. Sometimes a new melody is formed spontaneously, based on the composer's harmonic construction (or related harmonics).

At times this new melody is an inspired creation of unusual beauty. I am not speaking of an improvised solo, or a fast riff; but, of a new theme. Listen to Charlie Parker's version of *Embraceable You* by George Gershwin. The first chorus starts immediately with a new theme created by Charlie Parker based on the chord changes of *Embraceable You*. By the second chorus, he has developed the new theme into a soaring sequence of phrases that leaves the listener spellbound. This can be heard on the fourth cut of: *Charlie Parker All Star Sextet*, Roost Records. LP2210

The jazz piano man is an integral part of a combo. He plays background chords from which the lead instruments solo. Along with the bass and drums, he helps keep the rhythm going. When he has a solo, you will hear it in the right hand only. The left hand plays only an occasional chord (no rhythm) at the chord changes, leaving the right hand free to express the player's ideas.

Jazz introductions are often rehearsed and part of a theme is played for four to eight bars. Endings are also often rehearsed so that the musicians can end together.

The next few chapters consist of techniques to further your study of popular piano. Do not forget that you are only a beginner and that it is important to master the art of popular piano playing before you can possibly attempt to learn modern jazz.

CHAPTER 12
MODERN CHORDS AND RHYTHMS

Ninth Chords

A ninth chord is formed by the addition of a major third interval above a seventh:

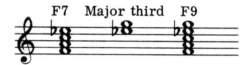

Ninths may be formed over any type of seventh chord, giving us these possibilities:

Ninths may be flatted or augmented:

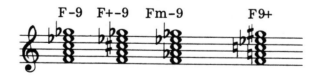

The root is often omitted when playing the right hand:

Ninth chords may be used in any position in the melody. The following examples illustrate various chord positions in the right hand. This chord is the most often used without any alterations.

For left hand positions of this chord see the Chord Index, pages 127—137.

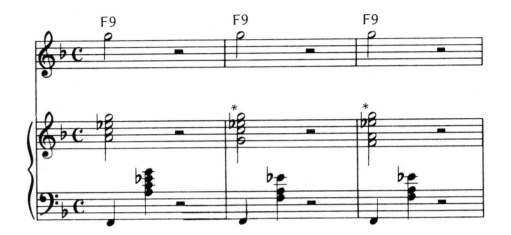

Eleventh Chords

To form eleventh chords, add a minor third above a ninth:

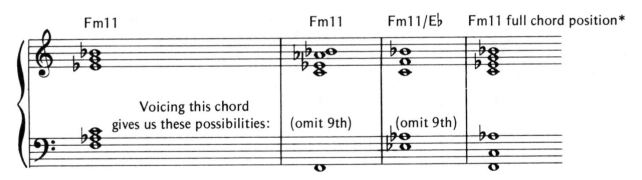

Note: Minor 11th chords have a minor triad.

*Beginners may omit these chords if too difficult.

To form augmented 11th chords, add a major third above a ninth.

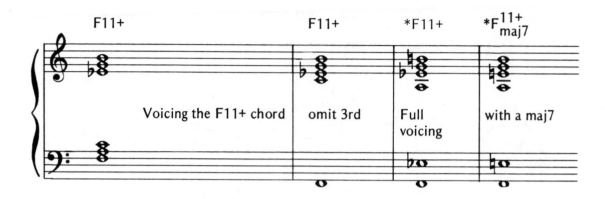

* Beginners may omit this exercise.

To accustom our ears to the sound of the sixth and ninth chord combinations, play over the following keyboard harmony progressions.

Flatted Fifth

The fifth of any seventh chord may be flatted for a more dissonant effect and is used with minor seventh chords;

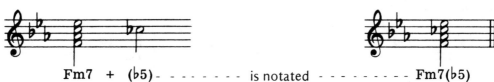

Fm7 + (♭5) - - - - - - - is notated - - - - - - - Fm7(♭5)

Other Seventh Chords

The following example illustrates seventh chords other than those we have studied:

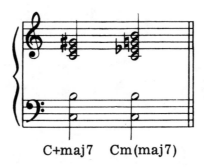

C+maj7   Cm(maj7)

Elevenths and Thirteenths

For added dissonance elevenths and thirteenths may be added to seventh chords:

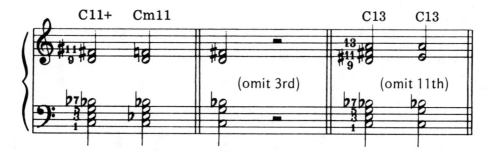

106

Modern Rhythms*

Some of the rhythms that can be substituted for the swing bass (page 62), are found in the following arrangements of *Red River Valley:*

Red River Valley

Traditional Cowboy Song

*Beginners can omit these examples on this page that are too difficult to play.

CHAPTER 13

MODERN SCALE FILL-INS

A song played without any variation in either the accompaniment or melody will sound monotonous. To eliminate this and to add to the general coloring of the song, we can improvise certain patterns, or fill-ins, in both the melody and the accompaniment. Chord progressions (pages 86—87) are among the many new harmonic devices that add tonal coloring. Now let us look at the possibilities for improvisations in the melody.

Melodic Improvisation Runs

The *pentatonic scale* consists of a major third, together with the sixth and ninth of the scale, and can be used in runs to vary sustained whole notes.

Generally, the scale can be used with any chord built on a major triad. Because the sixth and ninth are neutral in quality, they can be used to advantage for passing tones between the notes of a major chord.

The pentatonic scale may be altered for variety. However, alterations should be consistent. If we raise the second tone and lower the sixth we should do so consistently throughout the run.

Any rhythmic pattern may be used. Two rhythmic patterns that may be included in runs are:

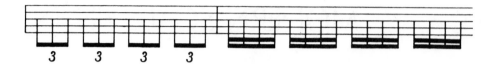

Melodic runs may also be built on the actual chord with passing tones inserted:

Let us now play the pentatonic scale using the fingering shown in the right hand. This time we will play in the *Key of F.*

Ascending:

Descending:

Practice the following scales for both the right and left hands. A few of
the scales in the keys most often found are:

Key of C (right hand):

Key of C (left hand):

Key of F (right hand):

Key of F (left hand):

Fill-in Possibilities with Pentatonic Scale

The left hand may be used for runs while sustaining or playing melody line in right hand.

a. Sustaining:

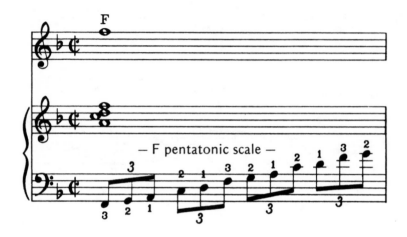

F pentatonic scale may also be used as a fill-in with either Fmaj7, F7, or F9 chords.

b. Playing melody line:*

*Beginners may omit this example.

Pentatonic scales can be used for fill-ins for the right hand by:

Sustaining the left hand a complete or half bar on a held note, and using a run in the right hand for a fill in.

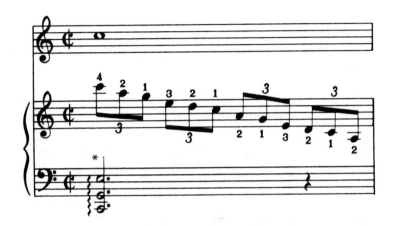

By playing over the preceding examples and the scale, you will accustom your right and left hands to the movement of this scale.

Use of the pentatonic scale in a song will be illustrated in Chapter 14.

For additional practice in pentatonic scales, see *Chord Index and Pentatonic Scales,* pages 127–137.

Exercises

Practice the following exercises.   If possible memorize the rhythms.

1. Play this left hand fill-in.   Be careful not to hop.   Play each note evenly.

*Beginners may play "C" octave position.

2. Play this rhythm, accenting the notes slightly on the second and fourth beats.

3. Play this rhythm smoothly. First play the left hand, then the right hand, then both hands together.

When you can play this in a smooth manner, go back to Exercise 2, then on to Exercise 3 without losing any beats.

Some Things to Remember

1. If, at this point, you have omitted practicing the songs or exercises so far, go back and review them. This is important as you will be playing a complete song in the next chapter.

2. Watch the fingering. Play as indicated, using the fingering marked. Do not attempt to use your own fingering.

3. The pentatonic scale we have just covered is important. Try to play it correctly.

4. When you hear recording artists playing the piano, do not try to imitate them. Remember, you are learning the art of popular piano playing. To play like a professional takes years.

5. Watch your posture and hand position. Sit straight; keep your wrists above the keyboard.

6. Chapter 14 is devoted to a complete popular song. Do you feel ready? Is there anything you have forgotten to review?

CHAPTER 14
PLAYING POPULAR MUSIC

Before we examine the procedure for playing popular music, it is important to observe the various *expression marks* used in popular (and classical) music. They include *dynamic marks* (degrees of volume), *tempo marks* (degrees of speed), and so forth.

Following is a list of some frequently used musical symbols, with their Italian meanings and English translations.

pp	*pianissimo*	- very soft
p	*piano*	- soft
mf	*mezzo-forte*	- medium loud
f	*forte*	- loud
ff	*fortissimo*	- very loud
◁	*crescendo*	- gradually louder
▷	*diminuendo*	- gradually softer
♩	*staccato*	- short
♩	*marcato*	- accented
accel.	*accelerando*	- gradually faster
rit.	*ritardando*	- gradually slower
⌢	*fermata*	- a pause or hold
♩ ♩ ♩	*legato*	- in a smooth, connected manner

Octave Marks 8·············⌐

When placed above the notes, the marks indicate that those notes must be played an octave higher; when placed below, an octave lower. The length of the marks indicates the number of notes to be played an octave above or below.

Procedure for Playing Popular Sheet Music

We can set down the procedure for playing popular sheet music in the following order:

1. Select a song that you would like to play. At this point try a song in an easy key such as F, C, G, E♭, or B♭. They are written out below for your convenience.

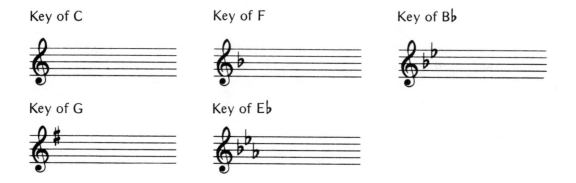

Key of C   Key of F   Key of B♭

Key of G   Key of E♭

2. Play the melody from the top treble clef—the single melody line with chord notations above it. Play either single tones or octaves in the right hand. With the left hand, change the chords where indicated. Do not at this point use any rhythm for the left hand. Just chord along as in the example below.

chord along - - - - - - - - - - - - -

Keep left hand within this range

3. Now get a good bass rhythm going in the left hand. We choose the left-hand rhythm according to the mood and style of song. For example, a swing bass may not go well with a disco song, but may be just right for a swinging blues song:

Often popular sheet music arrangements are quite easy. Most times they are over-simplified. A good swing bass played in even time will enhance many of the great standard songs of the past: *Ain't Misbehavin', Manhattan.* Other songs of a later period, *Alfie* and *Lady;* songs by Paul Anka and Marvin Hamlisch, have swing bass possibilities.

4. Be aware where held tones occur. It is here that we can use fill-ins with pentatonic figures, or compose our own breaks. When you acquire some playing experience, it will be easier to make up your own fill-ins.

5. A good bass line is important. As simple as a piano arrangement may be, it often indicates a bass line that has some value.

6. Next play the swing bass with the melody. Use a single tone in the right hand.

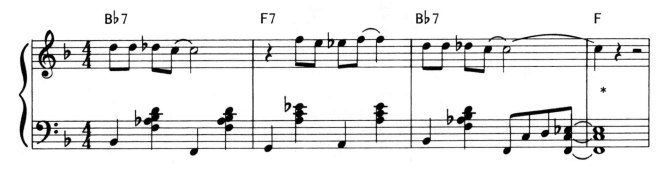

*Fill-in possibility here. We can use the F pentatonic scale as a basis for a fill-in:

F pentatonic scale

I will use the following break based upon the pentatonic scale. An Ab passing tone has been added. (Slide down with the third finger on Ab to G.)

7. Before playing the complete arrangement, we have to consider the right hand. Harmonies should occur on the strong beats of a song—in this song, the first and third beats. The other tones of the melody may be considered as passing or leading tones. This can be played with single tones. Therein, we "hang down" the harmonies from the top melody line. Keep the harmony simple and put in the important tones to achieve a full sound.

8. There are other possibilities such as consecutive thirds in the right hand:

octaves:

consecutive fourths:

These possibilities are illustrated in the last song of this book (*Going Home*).

We are now ready to play a full piano arrangement (four bars).

*Pick up first finger of right hand. (The D may also be omitted.)

9. Other considerations we will discuss are voicing the right hand in fourths, and filling in the octave. Fourths have a most contemporary sound when voiced in the left and right hands together. Remember, a fourth is formed by "hanging down" two and a half steps from melody line:

{ 2½ steps

interval of fourth

Play the exercise on the next page paying particular attention to fingering. Try to connect the fourths. Do not hop.

Exercise in fourths: (beginners can omit these exercises)

white keys

Parallel fourths:

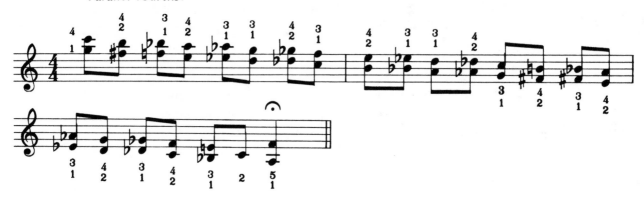

10. To fill in the octave, we merely add the missing tones of the chord between the octave tones:

In the last part of the song on the next page we have full octave voicing in the right hand. Practice the right hand separately. (Beginners can omit this.)

11. Finally, it should be remembered that sheet music is published for the pianist with a limited amount of musical training. In essence it is like a rough drawing sketch. It omits the substance of the composition and leaves it to the player to color in the sound and bring the picture into focus. In brief, it is up to you to bring your knowledge and musical sensitivity to a given song and try to make it sound like "something."

I have tried to show you, step by step, how to construct your own piano arrangements by applying the principles we have illustrated in the preceding pages. When you have gone through all the pages of this book and played the last song, you have actually only just *begun* to learn. Now is the time to buy sheet music of the great standards of the past in easy keys (F, G, C, B♭) and try to work up some arrangements. Because the music is "sketchy" and leaves much to the imagination, it is ideal for working out your own arrangements.

It is also a good idea to listen to recordings to find out how a particular song should sound. Rock and disco records often "sketch in" the basic left-hand beat for the piano, and subtle countermelodies and breaks. Play and listen to everything, then try to improve on it.

On the next page is a song I have arranged for you, based on a theme by Antonin Dvorak. Beginners should notice the instructions on a Fmaj7 chord, eight bars from the ending. If these next eight bars are too difficult, go back to the first eight bars, and end the song on the C6 chord.

Going Home

*Theme by A. Dvorak
Piano arrangement by Win Stormen

Ad libitum—not too fast, in a free manner

*Largo theme from *New World Symphony*

**Beginners may end on C chord the second time.

*If this left-hand chord is too difficult, play an octave position (C Chord), or single tone(low c).
**Beginners: D.C. means *Da Capo*—repeat from the beginning eight bars.

CHAPTER 15

IDEAS FOR SELF-STUDY

After outlining the basic principles for the self-study of popular music, I would like to offer some further suggestions for continuing your studies.

To begin with, it is a good idea (although not absolutely essential), to study classical music with a competent teacher at the same time that you study popular music. For example, a knowledge of No. 13 of J. S. Bach's *Two-Part Inventions* is good background for learning George Gershwin's "Summertime" from *Porgy and Bess*. The two works are in the same key, with somewhat similar chord progressions, except that the chords in the *Invention* open or spread out as in an exercise. If you opened up the chords in "Summertime," you could improvise a chorus *à la* Bach. If this astounds you, read on for another eye-opener.

Next, try improvising another chorus over "Summertime" *in your own manner*. If this sounds complicated, it is, since you have not reached this level of achievement. But if you had studied the classics, including the *Two-Part Inventions*, and had gone on to study popular music, you would have found such improvising both possible and stimulating.

A question that may arise in the reader's mind is: How far can I go *by myself* in the study of popular music? The answer is very far. As you develop your technique, you can learn new styles of playing. This book should be of great value to those without previous musical training. I hope that those with some training, popular or classical, have been able to assimilate *all* the material in this book. If so, I urge those who would like to go on to more advanced work to do so by all means.

Here, then are some areas of popular piano not included in this book that you might want to pursue. For example, variations of stride piano (left-hand swing bass) are almost a complete study by themselves; the Latin American beats for the right and left hands in such rhythms as the Bassa Nova, Reggae, Merengue, Cha Cha, and the almost forgotten Rhumba.

Since the left hand is the rhythm section of the piano for our purposes, we should have at our command many rhythms to embellish a song. Here are a few, that you may have heard at one time or another. One that is popular is rhythm and blues. In the days of the swing bands it was known as *the shuffle.* In the 1930's and 1940's, these rhythms were the musical trade marks of the Henry Busse and Jan Savitt swing bands. Later, Elvis Presley and Chubby Checkers re-popularized rhythm and blues as we know it today. Another early rhythm, *Pine Top boogie,* is a very special boogie woogie rhythm based on Pine Top Smith's piano style. Disco, Rock and Roll have a special way of playing the left hand as we have seen in this book. You may want to explore this further by looking at sheet music for disco and rock and roll arrangements of current favorites.

At one time the right hand and left hand were like horse and jockey. They started out together, stayed together during the race (in the piano, let us say the chorus), and finished together. The right and left hands were inseparable. Today, it is an entirely different story. In certain jazz piano styles the right hand is more important than the left (be-bop and modern jazz).

The right hand is today's sound for the jazz piano man. The melody line is frequently played in single tones and improvised upon with single tones and embellishments, all leading to a single tone melody line improvisation. In the old days we heard a clutter of chords with the right hand, with the left-hand stride piano or swing bass. The change is remarkable if one considers the contrast in the two styles. On the other hand, if you trace the development of styles from Ragtime to Modern Jazz, you will see that it all came about gradually, step by step, year by year, until it arrived at its present form.

In learning popular piano however it is a good idea to learn to play both hands together. When you study jazz, concentrate on the right hand. I have heard great jazz pianists, known for sensational right hands, who sometimes play with both hands together. For example, one night in a small café, I heard to my amazement Thelonious Monk playing a tune with both hands in the old swing bass style. Monk is noted for a terrific right hand, and to hear him play the old swing bass was indeed a surprise, for one rarely hears this on his records.

What style do you like? What style would you like to play? Who are some good exponents of these styles? It may be impossible to imitate your favorites by listening to records, but you will at least have a model and a goal in view. Often my piano students come to me and say: "I'd like to play like . . . . . ." Well, today there are so many styles, so many ways to play a song, my answer is always: *first, learn the basics.* This book is a start.

CHAPTER 16

POP PIANO KEYBOARD GRIP EXERCISES

The following exercises should be practiced as warm-ups, as preparation for learning a song, or just as a daily drill to keep your fingers in shape. You will find that when you do not play for some time, your fingers will be stiff. These exercises will help.

The first is a keyboard exercise to help your fingers grip the keyboard in a solid manner. It is designed to prevent hopping around, or a choppy technique, in the right hand.

This exercise is in whole notes. Play it in whole notes. Connect the sounds of each tone. The value of this exercise is to make sure you do this. Do not pick up your finger to play the next tone unless it is connected with the preceding tone. If there is a break in sound, repeat until there is none.

Repeat each line three times, rest, and then go to the next line.

Right Hand

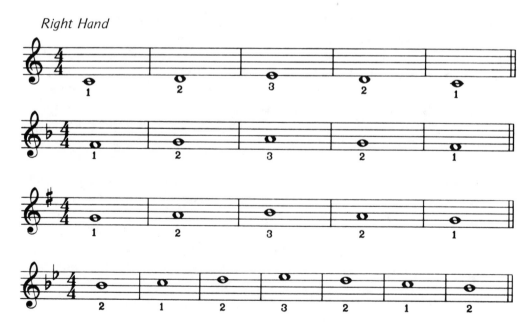

These exercises are ideal preparation for the jazz pentatonic scales in the last part of this book.

Popular Piano Scales

The following scales are a good warm-up for daily practice. Play 15 minutes a day to keep your fingers in shape.

ascending. . . . . pause and rest. . . descending

*tuck first finger below third

*tuck first finger below fourth

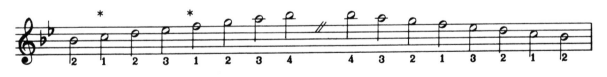

*tuck first finger

*tuck first finger

*tuck first finger

Chord Index

and

Pentatonic Scales

Major Chords

Right Hand

Left Hand (Rhythmic Bass)

*Bass Notes—Single or Octave

In general, where the bottom tone sounds too fuzzy, or the top tone is too close to the chord following, it may be omitted. Otherwise, you can play either a single tone or octave in the left hand first and third beats.

Minor Chords

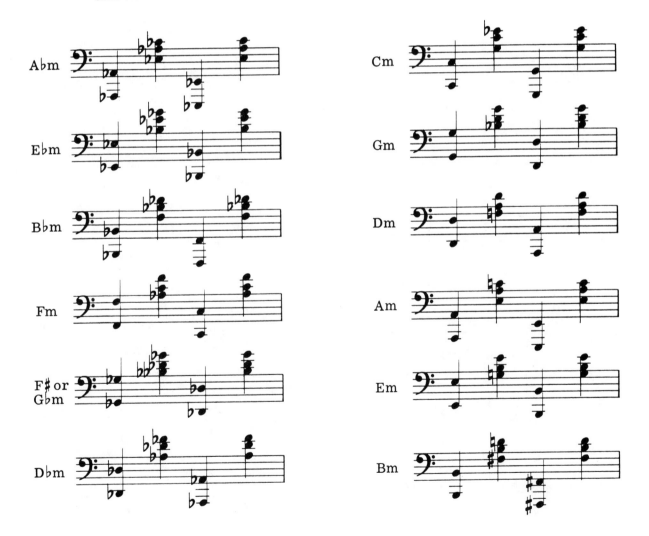

Seventh Chords

Right Hand

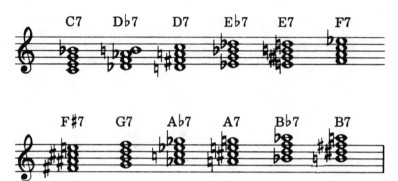

Left Hand

The following positions may also be used for ninth chords.

Augmented Chords

Right Hand

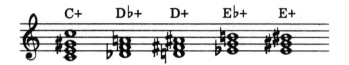

Left Hand

Minor 7th Chords

Right Hand

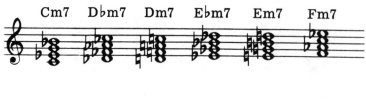

Left Hand

Major 7th Chords

Right Hand

Left Hand

Diminished 7th Chords

The following are three diminished chords commonly found in popular sheet music, together with their four possible letter names. Their spellings are those used in popular music:

Right Hand

Left Hand

Flat Fifth

The fifth of any seventh chord may be flatted for a more dissonant effect. This is frequently used with minor seventh chords.

Flatted Ninths

Ninths also may be flatted for added dissonance. Flatted ninths over major chords sound almost like diminished seventh chords:

Added Sixths

To major and minor triads we may add one whole tone above the fifth of the triad. This is called the "added sixth." The added sixth is of transparent, neutral sound quality.

Augmented 7th Chords

The 5th of any chord may be *augmented* with an added 7th:

Other Seventh Chords

The following example illustrates seventh chords other than those we have studied before.

Pentatonic Scales

(Left Hand)

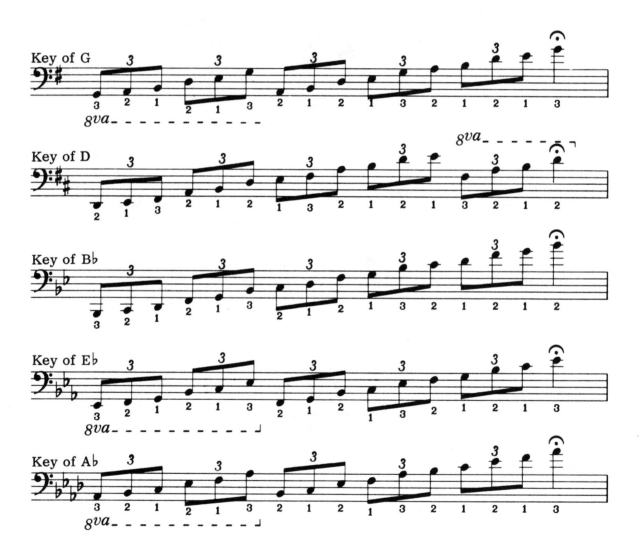

Pentatonic Scales

(Right Hand)